WORLD WAR II

From the Rise of the Nazi Party to the Dropping of the Atomic Bomb

Diane C. Taylor
Illustrated by Sam Carbaugh

Nomad Press
A division of Nomad Communications
10 9 8 7 6 5 4 3 2 1

This book was manufactured by Versa Press
East Peoria, Illinois
May 2018, Job # J17-12591

ISBN Softcover: 978-1-61930-657-8
ISBN Hardcover: 978-1-61930-655-4

Educational Consultant, Marla Conn

Questions regarding the ordering of this book should be addressed to
Nomad Press
2456 Christian St.
White River Junction, VT 05001
www.nomadpress.net

Printed in the United States.

Titles in the Inquire & Investigate Great Events of the Twentieth Century set

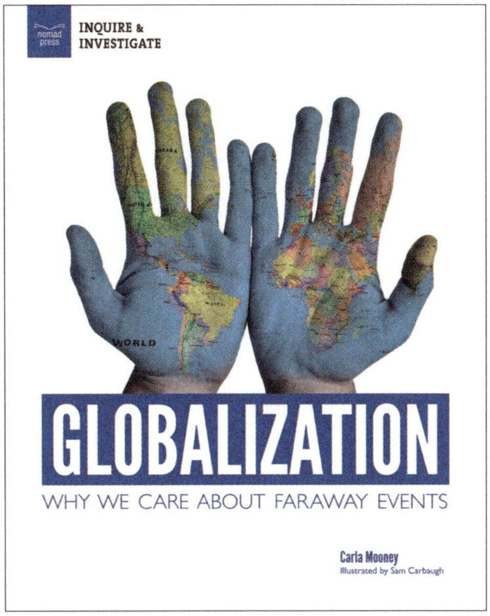

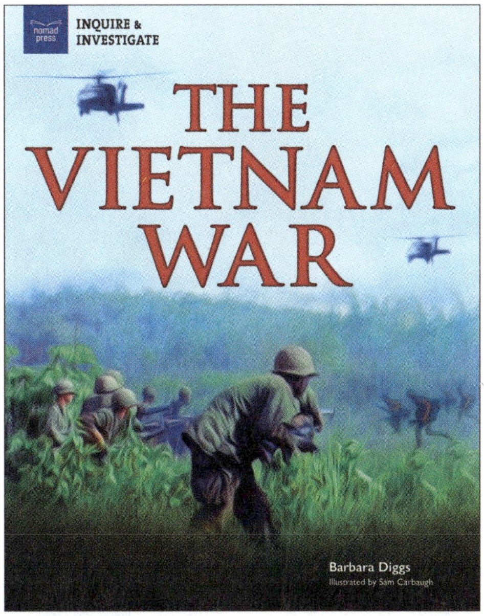

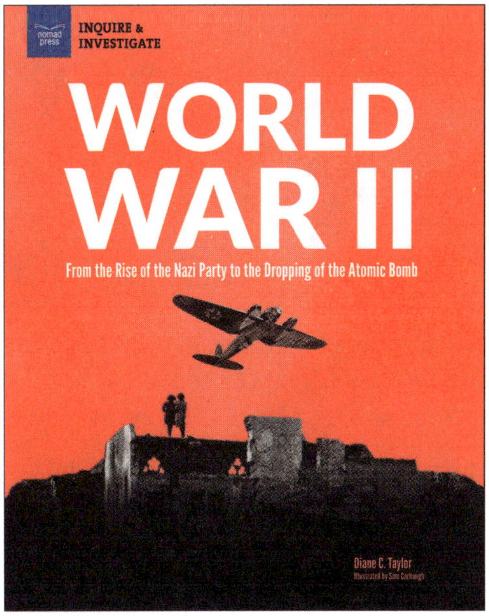

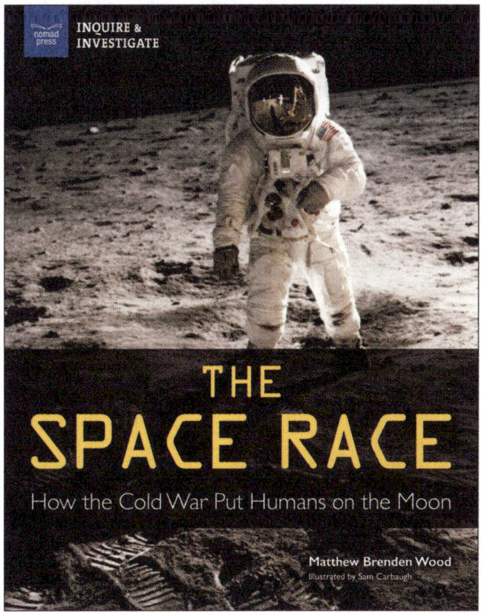

Interested in primary sources? **Look for this icon.**

You can use a smartphone or tablet app to scan the QR codes and explore more! Cover up neighboring QR codes to make sure you're scanning the right one. You can find a list of URLs on the Resources page.

If the QR code doesn't work, try searching the internet with the Keyword Prompts to find other helpful sources.

World War II

What are source notes?

In this book, you'll find small numbers at the end of some paragraphs. These numbers indicate that you can find source notes for that section in the back of the book. Source notes tell readers where the writer got their information. This might be a news article, a book, or another kind of media. Source notes are a way to know that what you are reading is true information that other people have verified. They can also lead you to more places where you can explore a topic that you're curious about!

Contents

TIMELINE

1914–1918........................ World War I occurs between the Allied powers and Central powers. More than 9 million combatants and 7 million civilians die.

1919................................. The Treaty of Versailles determines penalties Germany must pay for its actions in World War I.

1925................................. Benito Mussolini becomes the fascist dictator of Italy.

1926................................. Emperor Hirohito becomes the 124th emperor of Japan.

1928................................. Joseph Stalin becomes the communist dictator of Russia.

1931................................. Japan invades China.

1933–1934........................ Adolf Hitler becomes chancellor and president of Germany.

1938................................. Germany adds Austria to its territories and occupies Czechoslovakia.

September 1939............... Germany invades Poland. Great Britain, France, Australia, New Zealand, South Africa, and Canada—most of the Allied powers—declare war on Germany. World War II begins.

April 1940......................... The German conquest of Western Europe begins—Denmark, Norway, Belgium, the Netherlands, Luxembourg, and France all fall.

June 1940......................... Germany occupies Paris, France.

July–October 1940........... The Battle of Britain occurs, when Britain defends itself against Germany's powerful Luftwaffe.

September 1940............... Italy invades Egypt.

February 1941.................. Germany sends troops to Egypt to support their Italian allies.

June 1941......................... Germany invades Russia.

December 1941................ Japan bombs the American naval base at Pearl Harbor, Hawaii. The United States declares war against Japan the next day. The rest of the Axis powers—Germany, Italy, Hungary, Romania, and Bulgaria—declare war on the United States.

February 1942.................. Many Japanese Americans are sent to concentration camps in the United States.

TIMELINE

May 1943............................ German and Italian troops surrender to the Allies in North Africa.

July 1943............................ Benito Mussolini is deposed.

September 1943................ Italy surrenders to the Allies. Fighting continues in Italy between the Allies and the Germans.

June 1944.......................... More than 160,000 Allied troops invade the coast of Normandy, France, on D-Day.

August 1944...................... The Allies liberate Paris.

April 1945.......................... Benito Mussolini is executed by Italian partisans.
Adolf Hitler commits suicide in his bunker in Berlin, Germany.

May 1945........................... Germany surrenders.

June 1945.......................... The United Nations charter is adopted and signed.

August 1945...................... The United States drops atomic bombs over Hiroshima and Nagasaki, Japan.

September 1945................ Japan signs terms of surrender aboard the USS *Missouri*.

October 1945 .... The United Nations begins operations in New York City.

1947.................................. The United Nations partitions Palestine between Jews and Arab Palestinians.

1948.................................. Israel becomes an independent country.

1949.................................. The Soviets oversee the creation of communist German Democratic Republic (East Germany). In the west, the democratic Federal Republic of Germany is created. Berlin is divided between the two.

1961.................................. The Berlin Wall goes up between East and West Berlin, between the Soviet and Western sectors of the city.

October 1989 .... The Berlin Wall begins to come down. East Germans can once again cross freely into West Germany.

1990.................................. Germany becomes a unified country.

1993.................................. The European Union is formed.

genocide
persecution
turmoil
Blitz
conventional warfare
annihilation
dictator
infrastructure
isolationism
communism
conscientious objector
internment
nuclear bomb
anti-Semitism
Jew
Nisei
pacifist
prejudice
innovation
Eastern Front
precision bombing
disarmament
kaiser
kamikaze
annex
democracy
propaganda
immigrant
concentration camp
Luftwaffe
Third Reich
island hopping
No Man's Land
fascist
Nazi
casualties
atrocity
führer
Holocaust
Blitzkrieg
rationing
crematorium
industrialize
Bolshevism
reparations
armistice
Western Front
European Union
diplomacy
Marxism
refugee
boycott
ruthless
hostility
dictatorship
fanaticism
destabilization Axis powers
racial cleansing
radiation
mobilize
fallout
arson

Introduction

What Was the Second World War?

Why were there so many civilian deaths during World War II?

Because of the policy of total annihilation adopted by some nations during World War II, civilians had no protection against bombings, ground attacks, or mass killings. Many civilians also starved because of lack of food.

World War II was a global conflict that lasted for six years, from 1939 to 1945. It was an epic fight between two sets of countries. On one side were the Axis powers—Germany, Italy, and Japan. The Allied powers included Great Britain, the Soviet Union, the United States, and China. The war between the Axis powers and the Allies eventually caused the deaths of 60 million people, including 40 million civilians. What were these countries fighting about? What issues were worth the spilling of so much blood?

Two of the Axis countries were ruled by a dictator—Adolf Hitler (1889–1945) in Germany and Benito Mussolini (1883–1945) in Italy. Emperor Hirohito (1901–1989) and the Japanese military controlled Japan. On the other side, Great Britain was a democratic government with a prime minister, first Neville Chamberlain (1869–1940) and then Winston Churchill (1874–1965). The Soviet Union was a communist country ruled by the dictator Joseph Stalin (1878–1953).

The United States was a democracy with Franklin D. Roosevelt (1882–1945) as president. China's leader was a general named Chiang Kai-shek (1887–1975).

At first, these countries fought over the right of nations to be free from invasion. All of the Axis leaders hoped to expand their power by taking over other countries. Hitler and the Nazis wanted to control all of Europe and eventually the entire world. Mussolini wanted to create a Roman empire around the Mediterranean Sea. The Japanese military wanted to dominate Asia and the Pacific Ocean.

The Allied powers banded together to stop them.

As the war progressed, many more countries joined the battle—some joined the Axis powers while others joined the Allied powers. Eventually, more than 50 nations played some part in the war.

World War II was more than a conflict over just national boundaries. It became a fight to save an entire group of people. Adolf Hitler was an anti-Semite with an irrational hatred for people of the Jewish religion. He vowed to destroy all the Jews. He also wanted to wipe out other groups of people, including the Romani, Slavic peoples, and homosexuals. Hitler was stopped by the combined forces of the Allied countries.

THE SCOPE OF THE CONFLICT

No war has yet surpassed World War II in the number of lives affected by a conflict. World War II touched all four corners of the globe. In Europe, it started when Germany invaded Poland in 1939. Japan had already invaded China two years earlier. World War II spread to Africa, the United States, and throughout Asia.

PRIMARY SOURCES

Primary sources come from people who were eyewitnesses to events. They might write about the event, take pictures, post short messages to social media or blogs, or record the event for radio or video. The photographs in this book are primary sources, taken at the time of the event. Paintings of events are usually not primary sources, since they were often painted long after the event took place. What other primary sources can you find? Why are primary sources important? Do you learn differently from primary sources than from secondary sources, which come from people who did not directly experience the event?

BATTLE WATCH

The country that we now know as Russia was called the Union of Soviet Socialist Republics (USSR), or the Soviet Union, from 1922 to 1991. The city of St. Petersburg was called Leningrad during the Soviet era, named after the Soviet Union's first leader, Vladimir Lenin (1870–1924).

The war reached as far north as Alaska and as far south as Australia. It was fought in the Atlantic and the Pacific Oceans, across entire continents, and on tiny islands.

World War II was widespread in other ways, too. It impacted people's lives in ways that might be hard to understand today. For example, in many nations, food became scarce. Rationing was common. If you ran out of milk and bread, you couldn't simply buy more. No matter how much money you had, you had to wait until it was your turn to purchase those food items again. In some areas, such as Leningrad, Russia, there was so little food that vast numbers of people starved to death.

Many other consumer goods were in short supply, too. In the United States, for example, gasoline was so hard to get that it was rationed out at four gallons a week. Cars were not fuel efficient in the 1940s, so those four gallons didn't take you very far.

An American ration book from World War II

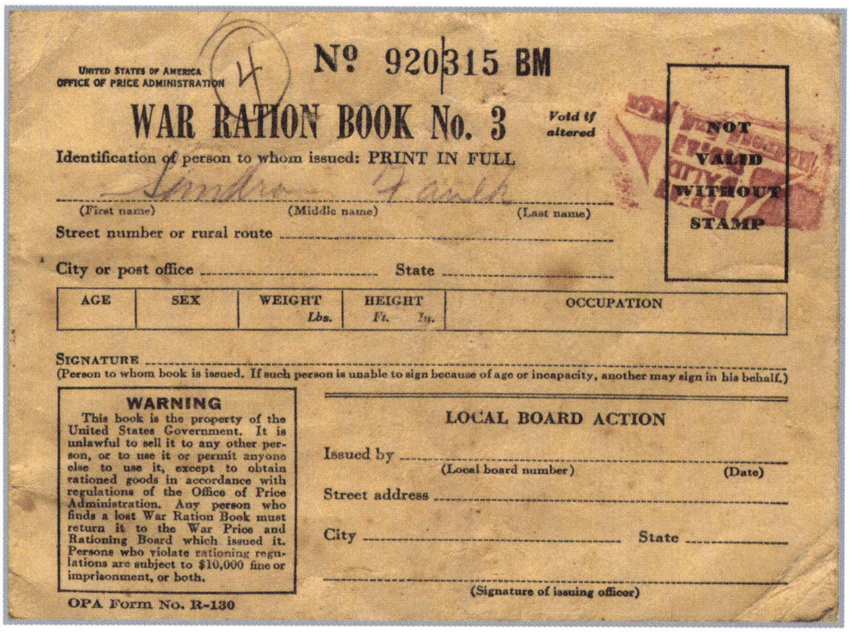

UNITED STATES OF AMERICA
OFFICE OF PRICE ADMINISTRATION

№ 920315 BM

WAR RATION BOOK No. 3

Void if altered

NOT VALID WITHOUT STAMP

Identification of person to whom issued: PRINT IN FULL

(First name) (Middle name) (Last name)

Street number or rural route

City or post office State

AGE	SEX	WEIGHT Lbs.	HEIGHT Ft. In.	OCCUPATION

SIGNATURE

(Person to whom book is issued. If such person is unable to sign because of age or incapacity, another may sign in his behalf.)

WARNING

This book is the property of the United States Government. It is unlawful to sell it to any other person, or to use it or permit anyone else to use it, except to obtain rationed goods in accordance with regulations of the Office of Price Administration. Any person who finds a lost War Ration Book must return it to the War Price and Rationing Board which issued it. Persons who violate rationing regulations are subject to $10,000 fine or imprisonment, or both.

OPA Form No. R-130

LOCAL BOARD ACTION

Issued by (Local board number) (Date)

Street address

City State

(Signature of issuing officer)

What changes would your family have to make in order to get by on four gallons of gasoline?

Millions of men's lives changed when they were drafted into military service. Women faced major changes, too. In many countries, women went to work in industries that would not normally have accepted them. They became machinists and mechanics, truck drivers and airplane pilots.

Millions of people lost their homes during World War II. Major cities were repeatedly bombed. If you lived in London, Berlin, or Tokyo, for example, you spent many nights in underground shelters while bombs exploded overhead.

When you emerged in the morning, you might find your house destroyed.

Worst of all was the plight of Europe's Jewish population. German soldiers removed millions of Jews from their homes, imprisoned them, and systematically murdered them in a campaign that eventually became known as the Holocaust.

NEW WAYS OF WAR

During World War II, tanks, airplanes, and submarines were some of the weapons that changed the way war was fought. Each had been used 20 years earlier during World War I, but only in limited ways. During World War II, these weapons took center stage.

When Germany invaded Poland, for example, people were shocked by the speed and power of the German tanks. No army had ever used such large numbers of tanks before. People heard them coming from miles away. The earth shook beneath their feet before the tanks even came into sight.

Imperial Ambitions

World War II came about, in part, because the Axis countries wanted to colonize other nations. But the Allied powers also owned numerous colonies. Great Britain had the most—it controlled almost all of India and had more than 10 colonies in Africa, too. In 1939, Great Britain had so many colonies, it controlled one third of the world's population. But they were hardly alone. France, Belgium, the Netherlands, and Spain also owned colonies in Africa and Asia. Even the United States had acquired foreign territories. During World War II, Guam and the Philippines were under U.S. control. Why did the Allies feel the need to prevent the Axis powers from colonizing other nations?

Airplanes were used in greater numbers and in new ways, too. They carried larger and more numerous bombs, and they could fly greater distances using less fuel.

VOCAB LAB

There is a lot of new vocabulary in this book. Turn to the glossary in the back when you come to a word you don't understand. Practice your new vocabulary in the VOCAB LAB activities in each chapter.

The deadliest new technology of World War II was the atomic bomb. On August 6, 1945, American pilots dropped a nuclear bomb over the Japanese city of Hiroshima. On August 9, 1945, they dropped another on the city of Nagasaki. Survivors of the attacks remember a brilliant flash of light, followed by a deafening explosion, and then a giant, mushroom-shaped cloud that rose up for miles into the sky. The bomb created a wind so strong, it ripped the clothes off people's bodies—even far away from the explosion site. The heat from the bomb was so intense, it burned people's flesh.

Atomic cloud over Hiroshima, taken from the bomber *Enola Gay*

credit: 509th Operations Group

A 13-year-old boy named Yoshitaka Kawamoto was sitting in a middle-school classroom half a mile from where the bomb went off. He survived, but most of his classmates died instantly. They were among tens of thousands who met a similar fate.

WARS OF TOTAL DESTRUCTION

Altogether, an estimated 60 million people lost their lives in World War II. The majority of those deaths—40 million of them—were of noncombatants.

We have already mentioned two reasons for civilian deaths: the use of deadlier weapons and the mass bombing of major cities. But the war tactics of two Axis powers—Japan and Germany—also added substantially to the civilian death toll. Neither country limited its killing to military personnel. They engaged in wars of annihilation, including the mass murder of noncombatants.

Japanese forces routinely killed civilians in their invasion of China. German forces deliberately killed civilians in their invasions throughout Eastern Europe and Russia.

Hardest to understand about the civilian deaths of World War II was the deliberate murder of 11 million Jews, Romani, and members of other groups. These deaths were an act of genocide—the destruction of an entire group of people.

BATTLE WATCH

Great Britain used more than 200,000 carrier pigeons to deliver messages behind enemy lines during World War II.

The Manhattan Project

The United States was the first country to create an atomic bomb. The research was conducted in secret under the code name Manhattan Project, in response to reports that Germany was working on an atomic bomb of its own. The Manhattan Project employed more than 130,000 people, including top scientists from around the world. Several had come to the United States to escape persecution in Germany.

Every war sees advances in weaponry. In its day, the horse-drawn chariot was a revolutionary innovation of combat. Today, it's the unmanned drone. What do you imagine weapons of war will look like 50 years from now?

German forces used several methods to murder Jewish civilians. They carried out mass executions, for example, and worked people to death through forced labor in prisons called concentration camps. Millions of Jews also lost their lives in specialized killing centers called extermination camps, which the Germans built in Poland.

The extermination camps were used in a factory-style approach to murder.

Hundreds at a time, Jews were locked into large chambers. When a poisonous gas was released into the room, everyone inside suffocated to death within 30 minutes. Their corpses were cremated, or burned to ashes, in crematoriums.

BATTLE WATCH

In 2017, the United Nations was involved in 16 peacekeeping operations around the world. The UN has sent personnel to African and Middle Eastern countries rocked by civil war and to countries recovering from natural disasters, such as earthquakes and hurricanes.

WAR'S AFTERMATH

After the war, in the wake of so much misery, many nations took steps to prevent such horror from ever happening again. Within months after the war ended, the United Nations (UN) came into being. The UN is an international organization dedicated to resolving conflicts through peaceful methods. The original UN charter was signed by 51 countries in 1945. Today, the UN has more than 190 member states.

Three years after the war ended, a new nation, called Israel, was created in the Middle East. Israel became a country that the Jewish people could call its own. Today, more than 6.3 million Jews live in Israel.

The present-day European Union (EU) also arose from the ashes of World War II. It was not fully formed until 1993, but it represents Europe's response to the devastation that resulted from the Second World War. The organization is founded on a pact among nations to live in political and economic harmony.

World War II caused death and devastation around the world, the effects of which can still be seen in today's political, geographical, and cultural climate. In *World War II: From the Rise of the Nazi Party to the Dropping of the Atomic Bomb*, you'll learn about the events of World War I that led to destabilization in Europe and sowed the seeds for another global conflict. You'll also read about Adolf Hitler and his agenda, the eruption of war in Europe, and the spread of war across the globe. Through eyewitness accounts, you'll come to understand the toll of this war on both individuals and countries.

In the next chapter, we'll take a look at the world's first global conflict and what World War I meant for the rest of the twentieth century.

KEY QUESTIONS

- **How might rationing have affected you and your family? What reasons other than war might countries have for rationing?**
- **Do you think there could ever be another world war? If you do, what do you think the conflict would be about?**
- **The United States is the only country that has ever used a nuclear weapon in war. In 2014, however, more than 10,000 nuclear weapons existed worldwide. Why do you think this is the case?**

A Personal Perspective

William L. Laurence (1888–1977) was a journalist working for *The New York Times* in the 1940s. He was in a support plane when the atomic bomb was released over Nagasaki on August 9, 1945.

"By the time our ship had made another turn in the direction of the atomic explosion, the pillar of purple fire had reached the level of our altitude. Only about 45 seconds had passed. Awe-struck, we watched it shoot upward like a meteor coming from the earth instead of from outer space, becoming ever more alive as it climbed skyward through the white clouds. It was no longer smoke, or dust, or even a cloud of fire. It was a living thing, a new species of being, born right before our incredulous eyes."[1]

Inquire & Investigate

VOCAB LAB

Write down what you think each word means. What root words can you find to help you? What does the context of the word tell you?

Allied powers, annihilation, Axis powers, dictator, genocide, Holocaust, Nazi, noncombatant, persecution, and **rationing.**

Compare your definitions with those of your friends or classmates. Did you all come up with the same meanings? Turn to the text and glossary if you need help.

To investigate more, compare maps from 1939 to 1945. How did boundaries change? What alliances were formed and what alliances disintegrated? How are maps a reflection of world events?

PLACES TO GO

If you don't know your way around the globe, World War II can be very confusing. Let's look at some maps.

Each of these websites shows a different map of the world during the time of World War II. You can refer to these as you read this book. You can also find historical atlases at your local library.

- **Take a look at the maps, and then see if you can answer a few questions.**
- **Map of Europe**
    - Which countries would you list as being in southern, eastern, western, or northern Europe?
    - Why was Germany considered a Central European country?

  Europe 1939 map

- **Map of Asia**
    - Which countries controlled which regions in Asia in 1939?
    - How large is Japan in relation to its surrounding neighbors?

  imperial powers 1939 map

- **Map of Colonial Africa**
    - How many different countries controlled Africa in 1939? Which countries had colonized the most land?
    - How might colonization have affected the outcome of World War II? Keep this question in mind while reading this book.

  map Africa 1939

Chapter 1

The First World War

How did the First World War lead to the Second World War?

When the globe was thrust into conflict between 1914 and 1918, Germany was blamed as a key player and forced to make extreme reparations. German resentment over the peace terms of World War I helped set the world up for another war only a little more than 20 years later.

To understand World War II, we need to return to the early 1900s and explore the causes and consequences of World War I. The Great War lasted four years, from 1914 to 1918. A horrific war, World War I set the stage for the rise of Adolf Hitler and the eventual plunge back into another brutal global conflict—World War II. Why were countries willing to go back to war so soon after the first one? How did half the world become embroiled in a conflict in the first place?

On the surface of things, World War I started in Europe when a man from Serbia killed the heir to the throne of Austria-Hungary while he and his wife were visiting the town of Sarajevo, Bosnia. Archduke Franz Ferdinand (1863–1914) and his wife, the Archduchess Sophie (1868–1914), were shot to death on June 28, 1914. A month later, in retaliation, Austria-Hungary declared war on Serbia.

And then came the domino effect. What started as a minor European incident escalated into an international disaster that involved more than 20 countries and killed more than 17 million people. A little more than 20 years later, the same countries fought again.

EUROPE AT THE TURN OF THE CENTURY

Compared to 100 years ago, Europe today is a far more peaceful continent than it used to be. Wars still break out, but that is the exception rather than the rule.

That wasn't always the case. European nations fought wars among themselves for centuries. They fought to gain territory, to control natural resources such as oil and iron ore, and to maintain access to the oceans in order to carry on trade with countries overseas.

After fighting a number of wars during the 1800s, European countries established a series of agreements among themselves as a way to protect themselves and keep the peace. They formed alliances and pledged to help one another if they ever found themselves at war.

The European system of alliances seemed like a good plan. But it all went terribly wrong, mostly because no country sincerely trusted its neighbors. Germany, in particular, made many people nervous.

BATTLE WATCH

Prior to World War I, European countries closely monitored the expansion of one another's railroads. Trains were the fastest way to move troops, so their expansion was seen as a threat.

The Blame Game

Immediately after World War I, most historians singled out Germany as the driving force behind the onset of the war. In recent years, however, many scholars have adopted a more balanced attitude. They say that Germany was certainly a big part of the problem, but that other countries were also responsible for what happened.

Christmas in No Man's Land

On December 24, 1914, fighting stopped along the Western Front when German soldiers in Ypres, Belgium, decided to celebrate Christmas. They lit candles around their trenches and started singing carols. Soon, soldiers in the British trenches were singing carols, too. Before long, men on both sides came out of their trenches and held an impromptu party in No Man's Land. They exchanged gifts of cigarettes, food, and alcohol, and gave one another souvenirs, such as buttons.

The spirit of Christmas spread across the Western Front and lasted, in some places, until New Year's Day. Altogether, around 100,000 British and German troops briefly put aside their differences until fighting started again in the new year.

By the turn of the twentieth century, Germany had grown rapidly in industrial and military might. The country's leaders bragged about how they planned to dominate Europe. For example, in 1911, a German general named Friedrich von Bernhardi (1849–1930) published a book called *Germany and the Next War.*

In it, he praised military aggression and said Germany had a moral duty to conquer others.

The title of the fifth chapter of his book boiled Germany's choices down to just two options: "World Power or Downfall."[1]

Bernhardi's book alarmed the European community. As Germany continued to ramp up its military strength, the country's ruler, Kaiser Wilhelm II (1859–1941), boasted in 1913 that he intended to invade France. Conflict seemed inevitable.

THE SPARK

By 1914, all of Europe seemed primed for war. The death of the Archduke Franz Ferdinand and Duchess Sophie was simply the spark that ignited the flame. On July 28, Austria-Hungary declared war on Serbia. In quick succession, the Russians mobilized troops against Austria-Hungary, Germany declared war on Russia and France, and Britain entered the war when Germany stormed through Belgium.

In 1914, Belgium was a neutral country with a national policy to avoid war. But even a neutral country defends itself. When Germany sent troops through Belgium, the small Belgian army fought back.

Germany had expected Belgium to let them simply pass on their way to France. Belgian resistance infuriated the Germans. In what became known as "The Rape of Belgium," they retaliated by killing civilians and destroying buildings.

Instead of providing protection, the alliances spread war to the far corners of the earth as countries took sides. On one side, there were the Central powers—Germany, Austria-Hungary, Bulgaria, and the Ottoman Empire, now called Turkey. They faced off against the Allied powers of Great Britain, France, Russia, Italy, the United States, and many more, including New Zealand.

Read eyewitness accounts of World War I at this website. How does a personal perspective change your understanding of the war?

PS

eyewitness to history World War I

Europe before the First World War

A War on Two Fronts

World War I had two main areas of action—the Western Front and the Eastern Front. We often hear more about the Western Front, where the fighting bogged down in trench warfare.

But the Eastern Front was important, too. That's where Germany battled the Russian Empire. The fighting there was more traditional and mobile—it never developed into a stalemate.

THE WESTERN FRONT

Most people imagined the war would last three to six months—at the most. In August 1914, Kaiser Wilhelm II announced to his departing troops that they would "be home before the leaves fall from the trees."

Just one year into the war, however, Central and Allied powers were lined up against one another in a stalemate. They faced off along a 500-mile area through France and Belgium that was called the Western Front.

German forces dug in on one side. French and British forces dug in on the other side. For the next three years, neither army gained a lasting advantage.

All along the Western Front, soldiers fought one another from trenches. At first, the trenches were little more than ditches. But as the stalemate dragged on, they became deeper and more elaborate.

Soldiers waiting in a trench

The trenches could be cold, cramped, flooded with water, overrun with rats, and infested with lice. Still, they developed into maze-like cities housing thousands of men at a time.

Between the two opposing systems of trenches lay a barren patch of ground called No Man's Land. This area could be hundreds of feet wide or just 20 feet wide. Regardless of its size, No Man's Land was a death trap. To engage in combat, soldiers rose up from their trenches and advanced toward the enemy, crossing No Man's Land. Out in the open, tremendous numbers of them were easily shot and killed.

THE GERMAN WAY OF WAR

The futility of trench warfare was not the only reason World War I dragged on for four years. The brutality of the German army also played an important role in prolonging the war. As German troops advanced through Belgium on their way to invade France, they killed thousands of innocent civilians and burned and looted villages.

One of the hardest hit places was Louvain. This was a village of historic significance, with a famous university and a library that had been in existence since 1426. German troops killed civilians and destroyed Louvain's cultural treasures, shocking the world and portraying themselves as enemies of civilization.

> Through terror and destruction, Germany's leaders had hoped to cow their enemies into submission.

Look at Louvain

The town of Louvain still stands, though nothing much from before 1914 is left. You can see the town and listen to the last living witness to the atrocities talk about her experience at this website.

Louvain video

Compare the scenes of modern Louvain with this footage from 1914. Is it recognizable as the same city?

Pathe Louvain

THE UNITED STATES ENTERS THE WAR

For three years, the United States avoided fighting in the war. Under President Woodrow Wilson (1856–1924), the country followed a policy of neutrality and focused on its own business without meddling in European affairs. But the United States couldn't stay on the sidelines forever.

In May 1915, German submarines attacked the British luxury cruise liner *Lusitania* off the coast of Ireland. The attack killed 1,198 civilians, including 128 Americans. The deaths of American civilians formed part of the rationale for the United States to enter the war.

In January 1917, despite prior assurances and agreements, Germany announced that it would resume sinking American ships in a policy of unrestricted submarine warfare. At the same time, the United States intercepted a cable known as the Zimmerman Telegram. In it they learned that Germany had proposed to help Mexico take back Texas, Arizona, and New Mexico—all parts of the United States.

When the Zimmerman Telegram was made public, Americans rallied to the defense of their country.

On April 6, 1917, America officially entered the war. It provided much-needed equipment and added more than 4 million fresh troops to the Allied cause. Still, it took about a year for those raw recruits to be trained for combat. By the spring of 1918, they were ready.

A Personal Perspective

American writer Richard Harding Davis (1864–1916) watched the German army march through Brussels, Belgium, on August 21, 1914. He wrote the following.

"At the sight of the first few regiments of the enemy we were thrilled with interest. After for three hours they had passed in one unbroken steel-gray column we were bored. But when hour after hour passed and there was no halt, no breathing time, no open spaces in the ranks, the thing became uncanny, inhuman. You returned to watch it, fascinated. It held the mystery and menace of fog rolling toward you across the sea."[2]

WAR'S END

Germany did not give up without a fight. On the Eastern Front, the 1917 revolution in Russia, led by a party called the Bolsheviks, resulted in an end to the fighting. In March, 1918, the new Bolshevik regime signed a treaty with the Central powers giving up a great deal of territory. Germany was free to concentrate its strength on the Western Front. In one last campaign—called the Spring Offensive—Germany threw everything it had left against the Allies.

It wasn't enough. By late September, the Central powers started to fall. Bulgaria went first on September 29, followed by the Ottoman Empire on October 30, and Austria-Hungary on November 3.

Germany was last to fall. In Compiegne, France, on November 11, 1918, Germany signed an armistice. It was an official admission of defeat along the Western Front.

French civilians, under German occupation for four years, welcome U.S. troops.

credit: Lieutenant Adrian C. Duff

African Americans in World War I

More than 350,000 African Americans joined the U.S. military during World War I. But the country—and the military—were segregated by race, so African American and white troops worked in separate units. One of those African American units was the 369th Infantry Regiment, or the "Harlem Hellfighters." These men fought as equals alongside French soldiers, and the French people honored 171 of them with their highest military award—the Legion of Honor, or *Croix de Guerre*.

RED POPPIES

Since 1919, November 11 has been a public holiday in many countries. It goes by several names—Armistice Day in Britain, Veterans Day in the United States, Remembrance Day in France. It's a solemn holiday, set aside to honor the fallen soldiers of war. Often, people wear red poppies on their clothes during Armistice Day celebrations. Poppies grow abundantly in Belgium and France, where fighting took place along the Western Front. Their red color has come to symbolize the blood of dead soldiers.

BATTLE WATCH

The Treaty of Versailles got its name because it was signed at the Palace of Versailles in Paris. Once, Versailles was the home of French royalty. Today, it is a popular tourist attraction.

THE TREATY OF VERSAILLES

In 1919, the Allied and Central powers gathered in Paris to hammer out the terms of Germany's defeat. France, Great Britain, and the United States were primarily responsible for determining Germany's fate. After so much death and destruction, the leaders of these countries were not inclined to be forgiving.

The Treaty of Versailles was a complex document—it included more than 400 articles. Overall, it had three main goals.

- To require Germany to pay for the damages caused in other European countries
- To severely limit Germany's military capabilities
- To deprive Germany of territory and colonies

The economic penalty came in the form of reparations, or money that Germany was required to pay in order to cover the costs of the damages caused by the war. The price tag to Germany came to 132 billion gold marks, or 33 billion U.S. dollars.

The military penalty demanded severe cutbacks in Germany's armed forces. The German army had numbered in the millions before the war, but the Treaty of Versailles now limited that number to 100,000 troops. Conscription—the drafting of men into military service—was outlawed. Limits were set on the number and types of weapons the country could buy or manufacture.

The land penalty deprived Germany of 25,000 square miles of territory it had taken from its neighbors in Europe.

In addition, every one of Germany's colonies in Africa and the Pacific Ocean was handed over to an Allied country, including to France, Belgium, Great Britain, New Zealand, and Japan. These countries would prepare the colonies for independence.

As Germany was being punished for its role in World War I, the 1918-1919 Spanish influenza epidemic was killing 20 million to 50 million people around the world. This was more than the number of deaths caused by the war. It made Europe even more unstable after the fighting stopped, as towns and villages in all major European countries struggled to rebuild infrastructure and take care of populations that had been devastated by both bombings and disease.

In the next chapter, we'll explore how Germany's post-war conditions would help nurture the rise of a powerful new political force—the Nazi party and Adolf Hitler.

KEY QUESTIONS

- What are some of the pros and cons of international alliances?
- Should the United States have joined the Allies in World War I earlier? Not at all?
- Which countries are allies of the United States today?
- Could a war the scope of World War I happen in today's society?

FEMALE WORKERS

With millions of men at war, great numbers of European women took on jobs formerly performed by men. In 1917, for example, female workers produced 80 percent of the munitions used in the British army. Women did the same work as men, but they received significantly less money. To protest their situation, some British women went on strike and received modest increases in pay. By 1919, their actions had resulted in a government report that supported the principle of giving women "equal pay for equal work."

Inquire & Investigate

POPULAR MUSIC IN WORLD WAR I

During World War I, many songs about the war became very popular. You can listen to some of them on YouTube.

great songs Great War

- **Listen to the songs and write a journal entry that responds to the following questions.**
  - Do the songs seem to be in favor of the war or opposed to it?
  - What is the overall mood of these songs? Are they upbeat, sad, angry?
  - Do the songs reveal anything about what the individual artist feels about the war?
  - How might these songs have helped people during the war?
- **Try composing some lyrics about war and setting them to music.** What challenges do you encounter?
- **Compare your responses with classmates or friends.**

To investigate more, listen to a variety of country music war songs of more recent years. How has the music changed in both substance and style? How has the music stayed the same?

war songs Boot

VOCAB LAB

Write down what you think each word means. What root words can you find to help you? What does the context of the word tell you?

alliance, armistice, domino effect, Eastern Front, reparations, retaliation, stalemate, treaty, and **Western Front.**

Compare your definitions with those of your friends or classmates. Did you all come up with the same meanings? Turn to the text and glossary if you need help.

POETRY OF WORLD WAR I

Both Wilfred Owen (1893–1918) and Edgar Guest (1881–1959) wrote poetry about World War I. But each man came to the topic from a different perspective. Owen fought in the war, while Guest did not, and each produced a different type of poetry.

- **Read both men's war poems at the following websites.**
  - Poems by Wilfred Owen
  - Poems by Edgar Guest

Wilfred Owen poems

Edgar Guest poems

- **Write a journal entry that responds to the following questions.** Then compare your responses with those of classmates or friends.
  - How does Owen's poetry make you feel? What he is trying to communicate about the war?
  - How do Guest's poems make you feel? What he is trying to communicate about the war?
  - Which poems did you like best, and why?
- **Try writing a war poem of your own.** How does the language you use reflect your feelings about war?

To investigate more, read the war poems of these other World War I authors. How do these poems compare to those of Owen and Guest?

Poetry Foundation WWI

LOST GENERATION

American writers who came to prominence after World War I, such as Gertrude Stein (1874–1946) and Ernest Hemingway (1899–1961), were known as the "lost generation." Their work explored the confusion many people felt in trying to understand what it meant to live a normal life in the aftermath of the most destructive war in human history.

Inquire & Investigate

ART OF WORLD WAR I

Wyndham Lewis (1882–1957), Paul Nash (1889–1946), and David Bomberg (1890–1957) were some of the artists who created paintings in response to their firsthand experience of World War I.

- **Study their paintings at the following websites.** Create a presentation in which you respond to the following questions.
  - What are the predominate colors in these paintings?
  - Are the images realistic, impressionistic, or something else entirely?
  - Are there any heroic figures portrayed?
  - What do you think these artists are trying to communicate about the war?

A Battery Shelled, by Wyndham Lewis

We Are Making a New World, by Paul Nash

File Sappers at Work, by David Bomberg

To investigate more, visit the website of the Metropolitan Museum of Art and watch a video about its collection of war-related art and art objects. How does the artistic portrayal of war differ between wars and artistic mediums?

Met war art

Chapter 2
Hitler's Rise to Power

How did Hitler seize such a complete level of power?

The German people struggled in the years after World War I, and Hitler was seen as an answer to many of the economic and social problems the population was experiencing.

During World War I, Kaiser Wilhelm II had promised Germany "a place in the sun." But defeat in this war cost Kaiser Wilhelm II the support of the German people, and before the armistice was signed on November 11, 1918, he had abdicated. He gave up his empire and went into exile in Holland.

In August 1919, the German monarchy was replaced with the democratic Weimar Republic and a new constitution. It was called the Weimar Republic because the people who created the constitution met in the town of Weimar.

Germany had a new constitution, and peace had come again to Europe.

It wouldn't last, however. During the next 20 years, wounded national pride, a ruined economy, and political turmoil in Germany would lead to renewed hostilities in Europe.

ECONOMIC COLLAPSE

An inglorious end to the war demoralized the German people. How might you feel if your country had been at fault for such a bloody conflict? The situation only grew worse as the country suffered an economic collapse. Germany had funded the war by issuing bonds. Now, those loans had to be repaid, even as the terms of the Treaty of Versailles further added to the country's debt.

> Germany could barely make ends meet.

What followed was a time of severe inflation. Prices for goods rose, while the purchasing value of money fell. Money became practically worthless. Imagine having $1,000 and being able to purchase only a penny's worth of food. People struggled to survive.

The German economy was just beginning to improve when it was rocked by yet another financial disaster—the Great Depression. When the U.S. Stock Market crashed in October 1929, economic troubles spread around the world. Germany, still reeling from economic catastrophe brought on by World War I, was hit especially hard.

Throughout these economic crises, German politics were in a state of chaos. No fewer than 40 political parties jostled for power in the German parliament, or Reichstag, but none of them was able to unify the country.

In the 1920s, the Nazi Party was just one of those dozens of political organizations, and Adolf Hitler was an obscure political figure. But the party and the man would soon merge and become the undisputed leaders of Germany.

The Swastika

The swastika was the symbol for the Nazi Party. Today, people around the world have very negative impressions of the swastika because of the violence associated with the Nazi Party. For most of its history, however, the swastika has appeared in many different cultures, where it represents positive qualities, such as the sun and prosperity.

BATTLE WATCH

Adolf Hitler was a decorated veteran of World War I. In all, he received seven commendations. The two he most often chose to wear were the Wound Badge and First Class Iron Cross.

Hitler's Austrian Background

Born in Austria in 1889, Adolf Hitler was not a natural-born German citizen. Yet he always considered himself more German than Austrian. He believed Austrians lived decadent lifestyles and were too tolerant of Jews. That's partly why he left Vienna for Munich when he was a struggling young artist.

HITLER'S EARLY YEARS

Adolf Hitler faced tough times in his early adult life. As a young man, he set out to become an artist, only to fail miserably. He found himself living in the grand Austrian city of Vienna in extreme poverty. He sometimes sought refuge in homeless shelters and accepted charity from family members just to survive.

By the time war broke out in 1914, Hitler had moved to Munich. He joined the Bavarian army, rose to the rank of lance corporal, and served as a message runner on the Western Front.

Adolf Hitler in the 1920s

After the war, he worked in a division of the Bavarian army intelligence and propaganda department. He gave speeches about nationalism, was against socialism, and spied on political parties. That's how Hitler became acquainted with the Nazi Party. He was spying on its members.

But as he spied, he discovered that he liked what they stood for—nationalism, racism, anti-Semitism. He believed that Germany was destined to rule the world. It made sense to Hitler that the German people must be racially pure. He also believed that Jews were to blame for most of Germany's problems.

Bavaria is a German state, located in the southeast of the country. Munich is the capital of Bavaria, in the same way that Austin is the capital of Texas.

HITLER'S POWERS OF PERSUASION

Do you ever wonder what people saw in Hitler? What makes someone a person that other people listen to, mesmerized?

> Hitler was a powerful public speaker, almost hypnotic in his ability to hold an audience's attention.

Representing the Nazi Party in its earliest years, he first spoke at small venues, with only about 100 people in attendance. Soon, however, he attracted crowds numbering in the thousands.

Hitler understood what many Germans wanted to hear. Constantly railing against the Treaty of Versailles, he exploited the anger many of them felt about their fallen position in the world. Hitler also inspired people with a vision of Germany as a strong and self-sufficient nation. Germany, he promised, would stand tall again.

Practice Makes Perfect

Hitler was a naturally gifted orator, but he also worked hard to perfect his craft. Sometimes giving three or more speeches a day, he rehearsed his mannerisms and choice of words. With practice, he learned to control the pace of his speeches, starting slowly and building to an emotional peak that pulled people to their feet. Is how you say something as important as what you say? Why or why not?

THE NAZI PARTY OF SOCIAL CHANGE

Hitler's nationalist messages gave hope to many struggling Germans. As a result, Hitler and the Nazi Party steadily grew in popularity. Styling themselves as the "Community of the People," Nazis gave out free food, created jobs, staged festivals, and organized neighborhood work groups.

The Nazi Party focused special attention on young people. Nazi leaders created youth groups for teenage boys and girls to learn the values of physical strength, racial purity, and love of country. Young people were taught to think of themselves as soldiers, defending the German way of life. They were called the Hitler Youth.

Every year, thousands of Hitler Youth attended a national rally, where the highlight was a nighttime speech by Adolf Hitler. Under the glow of burning torches, the youth fell under his spell and became some of his most loyal followers.

THE NAZI PARTY OF ANTI-SEMITISM

The Nazi Party was never just a movement about positive social change, despite its support of local communities. From the beginning, it preached a message of hate. Its main target was people of the Jewish religion. Hitler became the ultimate spokesman for anti-Semitism.

Germany (and much of the rest of the world) had a long history of blaming a small Jewish minority for the world's problems. Hitler tapped into that historical prejudice.

The Nazi Party of Racial Purity

Racial purity was a central part of the Nazi Party platform. The Nazis glorified the Aryan race, or non-Jewish people of Germanic and Nordic heritage. They thought every other race was weaker, less loyal, not as smart, and a drain on German resources. For the country to thrive, the Nazis said, every form of physical and mental weakness had to be weeded out.

When the Nazi Party controlled Germany, interracial marriage was outlawed. Male homosexuals were treated as criminals. Physically and mentally disabled children were sent to clinics and killed through starvation or overdoses of medicine. Jewish and Romani people were forced into concentration camps and murdered. Horrific acts were performed in the name of racial cleansing.

In a speech he delivered in 1939, for example, Hitler said Jews spread "infectious political and physical diseases." He said inflation was "instigated and carried through by Jews." He called Jews an "alien race." He said that communist rule in Russia—Bolshevism—was a "victory of Jewry." He predicted the "annihilation of the Jewish race in Europe."[1]

Hitler gave such speeches countless times. They were routinely met with thunderous applause.

CHANCELLOR OF GERMANY

How did a man who promoted such terrible ideals become the beloved führer, or leader, of Germany? He did it, in part, with the support of the German people. Hitler was a tireless and effective politician. He campaigned constantly for the Nazi Party. By 1933, the German people had elected more than 200 Nazi politicians to the Reichstag.

But when Hitler became chancellor on January 30, 1933, it wasn't because of an election. He came to power when the current chancellor resigned and the president, Paul von Hindenburg (1847–1934), appointed Hitler to take his place.

> Hitler did not so much seize power as have it handed to him. But to become a dictator, he resorted to political manipulation and violence.

On the night of February 27, 1933, the German Reichstag was set on fire, and the magnificent building burned through the night. The Nazis claimed the act of arson was part of a communist plot to overthrow the government. But some believed it was the Nazis themselves who set the fire so the party could justify its violent reaction.

KRISTALLNACHT

One of the most famous acts of anti-Semitism took place in Germany during the course of two days in November 1938. Throughout the country, Hitler's followers destroyed more than 270 synagogues, falsely arrested more than 30,000 Jews, killed more than 100, and vandalized Jewish businesses, homes, and hospitals. When the violence ended, shards of glass littered the streets. The event became known as Kristallnacht, which means "Night of Broken Glass."

German Reichstag on fire, February 27, 1933

credit: National Archives

BATTLE WATCH

The Nazi regime was called the Third Reich, or Third Empire. Hitler came up with the name based on his belief that he was leading a third German empire. He predicted the Third Reich would last 1,000 years.

As chancellor of the coalition government, Hitler outlawed the Communist Party and ordered a band of Nazi strongmen called the Sturmabteilung (SA) to intimidate, arrest, or murder the politicians of other parties. Then, with the competition eliminated, Hitler called for parliamentary elections. The Nazi Party was elected to a majority in the Reichstag.

Once Hitler had convinced many German politicians that the Communist Party was on the attack, Hitler had the government vote on a measure called the Enabling Act. This was an amendment to the Weimar Constitution that gave almost unlimited power to the chancellor and his cabinet in times of national emergencies. On July 14, the cabinet banned all political parties except the Nazis.

Hitler saluting a parade of troops in 1935

credit: Charles Russell Collection, NARA

The only thing that now stood between Hitler and total control was his co-leader—President von Hindenburg. But von Hindenburg died of lung cancer on August 2, 1934. Within weeks, Hitler held a special election. He asked the German people to decide if they wanted to combine the role of president and chancellor. They voted "yes" in overwhelming numbers.

Now Hitler was fully empowered to enact the policies of the Nazi Party—to eradicate the Jewish people and begin to exert German control over Europe.

PERSECUTION OF THE JEWS

The Nazi quest to eliminate the Jewish people didn't happen all at once. Instead, it was gradual. With each loss of their civil rights, Jewish people adjusted to a change in their circumstances, and hoped that their plight would soon improve.

Here are some of the first steps Hitler took to eradicate Jews.

- Called for a national boycott of Jewish businesses.
- Barred Jews from working as lawyers, college professors, and doctors.
- Enacted the Nuremberg Race Laws, which called for the "Protection of German Blood and German Honor."
- Banned Jews from public schools.
- Seized all Jewish savings.
- Required Jews to identify themselves in public with a yellow Star of David on their clothing.

A Personal Perspective

D.Sefton Delmer (1904–1979) lived in Berlin, where he witnessed the burning of the Reichstag on February 27, 1933.

"Five minutes after the fire had broken out I was outside the Reichstag watching the flames licking their way up the great dome into the tower. . . . After about 20 minutes of fascinated watching I suddenly saw the famous black motor car of Adolf Hitler slide past, followed by another car containing his personal bodyguard. I rushed after them and was just in time to attach myself to the fringe of Hitler's party as they entered the Reichstag. Never have I seen Hitler with such a grim and determined expression. His eyes . . . were almost bulging out of his head."[2]

You can read his account of the fire at this website.

Delmer eyewitness

Jewish people clung to hope even when the Nazis told them they were being "resettled." Few comprehended that they were headed toward concentration camps and killing centers. Despite evidence to the contrary, many people believed that Germany was still a civilized country. They believed, or at least they hoped, that the madness would end.

FASCISM

Fascism is a form of government that considers the nation more important than the individual. It maintains total control over its citizens' lives. Like the other Axis powers during World War II, Nazi Germany was a fascist government.

PREPARATIONS FOR WAR

On the military front, Hitler brazenly defied the terms of the Treaty of Versailles. Military service became mandatory and the country underwent a massive rearmament. Germany churned out panzers, the tanks for which the German army—or Wehrmacht—would become famous during the war.

The Allied powers of World War I knew that Hitler was not abiding by the Treaty of Versailles, but they did little to stop him. In 1938, Hitler sent German troops into Austria and annexed the country for Germany. Most Austrians probably favored unification with Germany. The Allied powers did not intervene.

Later that same year, Hitler planned to invade and occupy Czechoslovakia. At the last minute, he pulled back and, after weeks of negotiation, the Munich Agreement was signed by Germany, Great Britain, France, and Italy. In this agreement, the Sudeten area of Czechoslovakia, where about 3 million people of German origin lived, was given to Germany to avoid war. The Allies would not take military action and German annexations would be limited to Austria and Czechoslovakia.

Allied leaders realized too late that when Hitler said he was going to expand his empire and destroy the Jews, he meant it. In the next chapter, we'll take a look at the start of World War II in Europe.

KEY QUESTIONS

- **How did Germany's condition after World War I make it easier for people to support a dictator?**
- **Not everybody in Germany was an anti-Semite. Do you think they could have prevented the persecution of the Jews?**
- **What part did fear play in Hitler's rise to power?**

NATIONAL IDENTITIES

Every country has a collective sense of itself as a nation. When you think about the identity of the United States, what comes to mind? Who are we as a people? What values do we embrace?

- **Write a brief statement or create a presentation about the national identity of the United States.**
    - When do you feel proud to be an American?
    - Are there incidents from American history that make you uncomfortable?
    - What evidence supports your view of the national identity?
- **Share your statements or your presentations with your classmates or friends.** How do your concepts of national identity differ from one another?

To investigate more, read a newspaper or news magazine and find articles or editorials related to current affairs in the United States. How do these news pieces influence what you think about the United States? How do you imagine people outside of the United States might respond to these same articles?

VOCAB LAB

Write down what you think each word means. What root words can you find to help you? What does the context of the word tell you?

abdicate, **annex**, **anti-Semitism**, **Aryan**, **fascism**, **führer**, **nationalism**, **orator**, **propaganda**, **racial cleansing**, **racism**, **rearmament**, **socialism**, **swastika**, and **Third Reich**.

Compare your definitions with those of your friends or classmates. Did you all come up with the same meanings? Turn to the text and glossary if you need help.

Inquire & Investigate

POLITICAL INSTABILITY

Why would the German people vote to make Hitler both president and chancellor? From 1919 to 1932, 14 different men served as chancellor. That's more than one new leader a year. What might that be like in the United States? If the president changed every year, might Americans take drastic steps to form a more stable government?

HITLER AS AN INSPIRATIONAL ORATOR

The following YouTube video is a 10-minute compilation of Hitler speeches. They include English subtitles so you can understand what he's saying.

Hitler speeches video

- **Watch the video and pay close attention to the content of Hitler's speeches.**
  - Can you identify any important themes?
  - Do any of his ideas seem to have value?
  - What do you make of his body language?
- **Create two lists, one showing what you liked about Hitler's speeches, another showing what you didn't like.** Which list is longer, and why?

To investigate more, listen to the 12-minute speech British Prime Minister Winston Churchill delivered to the House of Commons on June 4, 1940. Churchill, too, was considered a great orator who inspired his followers. In this address, Churchill is responding to the Allies' recent defeat on the beaches of Dunkirk, France. Listen closely and respond in a journal entry.

Churchill speech 1940

Do you feel inspired? Reassured? Confused? How does Churchill's style differ from Hitler's?

THE OTHER NAZI LEADERS

Adolf Hitler is regarded as the driving force behind World War II and the Holocaust, but he did not rise to power alone. Who else contributed to the success of the Nazi Party and the death of so many people?

- **Using the internet and your public library, do some research on the following Nazi leaders:** Heinrich Himmler (1900–1945), Joseph Goebbels (1897–1945), Hermann Göring (1893–1946), Albert Speer (1905–1981), Joachim von Ribbentrop (1893–1946), and Martin Bormann (1900–1945).
- **Create a biographical sketch of one of these Nazi leaders and present your findings to your classmates or friends.**
  - What was his role in the Nazi organization?
  - What were his main Nazi accomplishments?
  - What kind of a relationship did he have with Hitler?

To investigate more, research some of the attempts German people made to thwart Hitler's agenda. Not everyone in Germany supported the Nazi Party. How did they resist? Why did their efforts fail?

THE MUNICH AGREEMENT

When England, France, Italy, and the United States signed the 1938 Munich Agreement, they engaged in an act of appeasement. They gave Hitler a portion of Czechoslovakia, hoping to prevent a more widespread European conflict. In hindsight, the Munich Agreement seems terribly misguided. But at the time, most people approved of it. In 1938, no one wanted another war, and few people understood the full scope of Hitler's intentions. Even Winston Churchill, never a friend of Hitler, said the Munich Agreement was for the best.

Chapter 3
The War in Europe

How did World War II unfold in Europe?

In addition to invading Poland, France, and Britain, and attempting to take over Russia, the Nazis carried out a systematic murder of the Jewish people, going as far as to ship people to killing centers.

On September 1, 1939, a beautiful, late summer day in Poland, the German military set in motion Adolf Hitler's plans to dominate Europe and exterminate the Jews. They started by invading Poland, their neighbor to the east. Immediately, the army established itself as a formidable and merciless force.

The Germans took over the country in just four weeks. They also introduced a new military tactic—air strikes combined with a simultaneous use of tanks. Stuka dive bombers appeared suddenly in the sky, dropping bombs on military targets or sweeping down low and firing on civilians. German tanks, the panzers, raced across the countryside at speeds and in numbers never witnessed before.

The onslaught of the bombers and panzers was so dramatic, journalists created a new word for it. They called it blitzkrieg, which is German for "lightning war."

WAR ON CIVILIANS

The invasion of Poland was shockingly brutal. As they had done during World War I, German troops laid waste to entire villages and murdered civilians. Jewish people, in particular, were singled out for humiliation and destruction. German soldiers dragged families from their beds during the night, lined them up against walls, and shot them. They hung Jews in public squares and beat them in the streets.

After Poland, German forces headed north, roaring through Denmark and Norway. They moved west to the Netherlands, Belgium, Luxembourg, and France.

BATTLE WATCH

When Germany overran his country, French General Charles de Gaulle (1890–1970) fled France for London, where he established the Free French Forces. De Gaulle's troops fought with support from the Allies.

Everywhere the Germans went, occupation was followed by the systematic killing of innocent people.

Marshal Petain

During its occupation of France, Germany divided the country into two political regions. German administrators governed the north. French administrators, under German authority, governed the south. The town of Vichy was the capital of that southern regime, which was led by Marshal Philippe Petain (1856–1951), a renowned veteran of World War I. With near dictatorial powers, Petain promoted regressive policies, such as depriving women of their independence and limiting workers' rights. Petain's government was also openly anti-Semitic, sending thousands of French Jews to their deaths in the extermination camps.

It took less than a year for Hitler's forces to bring most of Western Europe to its knees. Their crowning glory was the occupation of Paris. Germany occupied the capital of France on June 14, 1940.

FIRST RESPONSES TO GERMAN AGGRESSION

France and Great Britain were allies of Poland. Two days after the invasion, both countries declared war on Germany and vowed to combat their common enemy together. Just as in World War I, countries went to war because of the alliances they had made. Like a wave of falling dominoes, the conflict began to spread.

Compared to Germany, however, neither France nor Great Britain was fully prepared for combat. World War I had been fought on their territory and another war was inconceivable. It took time to mobilize troops and coordinate a plan of action. In that first year of the war, Allied delays and miscommunications allowed German leaders to rack up victories with remarkable ease. After Hitler occupied France in June 1940, he figured he would quickly overpower Britain as well, and then take Russia.

But events didn't unfold according to Hitler's plan. Part of the reason was geography. As an island, Britain was not vulnerable to an overland blitzkrieg-style invasion of tanks and artillery.

Hitler would have to take the country either by sea or by air, and the strength of Britain's naval fleet and its Royal Air Force blocked both of those options.

THE BATTLE OF BRITAIN

Unable to stage an invasion of Britain, Hitler decided to unleash a bombing campaign instead. He intended to crush the will of the English people and force their leaders to sign an armistice.

The German Luftwaffe showered bombs over Birmingham, Coventry, and Liverpool. For more than 50 days in a row, it bombed the city of London, the nation's capital. These air raids, known as the Blitz, mostly took place at night. With bombs hurtling from the sky, Londoners sought shelter wherever they could.

Londoners during the Battle of Britain

credit: National Archives

A volunteer looking for German aircraft during the Battle of Britain

credit: National Archives

Many people spent their nights in the London Underground, the extensive subway system below the streets of London. People slept on crowded station platforms, on trains, and in some service tunnels. Others sought refuge in the basements of homes and other buildings. The majority of people, around 60 percent, simply stayed home.

Large-scale evacuations of the cities were also carried out, especially for children. In an operation called Pied Piper, the British government relocated children to rural areas of England and even overseas to countries such as Canada, South Africa, and Australia. During the first four days of Pied Piper, about 3 million people were relocated.

PS

Visit this website and listen to British pilots recount their battles against the Luftwaffe.

battle Britain pilots' stories

The Blitz killed or injured tens of thousands of British citizens, and destroyed or damaged countless buildings. Still, the Luftwaffe failed to demoralize the people or force their leaders to capitulate. For the most part, Londoners went about their affairs with remarkable grace and determination.

Why? How did the people of London stay so resilient? What made them persist in going about their daily lives even as parts of their city were made unrecognizable because of the destruction?

To a large extent, the British people took courage from the actions and words of their leader, Prime Minister Winston Churchill. Churchill never abandoned the capital. He walked the shattered streets and rallied his people to carry on with confidence, even in their darkest hours. In June 1940, when Germany seemed unstoppable, Churchill proclaimed that the island nation would never surrender.

The British people stood strong against their invader.

Britain was not the only country to endure bombing throughout the war in Europe, nor was it the country that suffered the most from massive bomb attacks in Europe. That distinction goes to Germany.

From June 1943 to April 1945, the United States and Britain waged a bombing campaign over Germany called the Combined Bomber Offensive (CBO). The Allies' goals were to weaken Germany's industrial capability to wage war and to demoralize the German civilian population. The CBO raids lasted longer than the Blitz, claimed more lives, and resulted in more damage to German infrastructure.

BATTLE WATCH

Winston Churchill was a popular leader during the war, but in the years before, many had considered him reckless. He had a reputation as a warmonger—someone who would get the country needlessly involved in a war.

Music of World War II

Music and dance helped people cope with the stress of war. Do an internet search for the phrases below to listen to some of the most popular songs of the time. What is it about the music that might help people during war? Can you find samples of war music from other conflicts? How is that music both similar and different?

"Boogie Woogie Bugle Boy"

"Lili Marlene"

"Sing, Sing, Sing"

Dancing to swing music

In the Russian campaigns, skis were an important piece of military equipment. Russian troops, especially from Siberia, were formed into ski patrols. They were prized for their ability to move quickly across the frozen terrain. Imagine how fighting would have been different if they'd had to march instead of ski!

Explore the Siege of Leningrad with these firsthand accounts.

eyewitness Leningrad

THE CAMPAIGN AGAINST RUSSIA

At the start of World War II, Russia was Germany's most important ally. Joseph Stalin, Russia's communist leader, worked hand-in-hand with Adolf Hitler, assisting in his efforts to invade Poland. In August 1939, the two countries had signed the German-Soviet Pact, in which they agreed to trade German manufactured goods for Soviet raw materials.

German troops marching into Russia

credit: Johannes Hähle

Even more importantly, it was a nonaggression agreement: Each promised not to attack the other. Germany had invaded Poland from the east in September 1939 without fear of Soviet intervention. Shortly afterward, during that fall, the Soviet Union invaded Poland from the west.

> Because of their agreement, Stalin believed that Hitler would leave Russia in peace.

But under the policy of *lebensraum*, which means, "living space" in German, Hitler had long promised his followers that Russia would become a colony to support German expansion. He had always intended to invade Russia. When he did, in June 1941, Stalin reluctantly became one of the Allies.

As had happened in Western Europe, German forces at first swept across the country with relative ease. Despite a heavy counterattack by the Soviets in August and September, the German army reached the outskirts of Moscow in October 1941. Hitler boasted to cheering crowds in Berlin that Russia was on the brink of surrender. That proved to be a serious miscalculation.

The rains fell on Russia, creating deep fields of mud. Exhausted German forces ground to a halt in the mire outside Moscow. Then, the Russian winter set in. Oil in German tanks and trucks froze, leaving the armies unable to move either forward or backward.

Food could not be transported from the back lines to the men at the front. Many soldiers starved to death. Plus, assuming an early victory, Hitler had sent his soldiers into Russia without winter clothing. Now, his men froze.

Resistance

Throughout the war in Europe, individuals and small groups in all the occupied countries undermined Germany's military success. They damaged railroad tracks and bridges to disrupt the transport of German troops. They passed information to Allied leaders about the strength and whereabouts of Axis forces. If forced to perform services for the German invaders, they worked as slowly and poorly as possible.

Other resistance groups were large and highly organized. The Polish Home Army had a force of 400,000 soldiers. They fought numerous armed battles and staged an uprising in Warsaw. Likewise, hundreds of thousands of patriots in the French Resistance played important roles in the Allied invasion of Normandy. They went on to fight alongside Allied troops as they reclaimed Europe.

In the spring of 1942, German forces regrouped. But it was too late. The winter delays had given Russian leaders the time they needed to get their military and civilian forces prepared for combat.

In the battles that followed, the Russian people lost the lives of 27 million military personnel and noncombatants. Two million were killed, wounded, or captured in the battle of Stalingrad alone. Hundreds of thousands starved to death during the Siege of Leningrad, which lasted almost two and a half years.

> Still, the Russian people did not surrender. The stand they made against Nazi Germany played a crucial role in eventually bringing the Allies to victory.

A Personal Perspective

Russian writer Aleksandr A. Fadeyev (1901–1956) observed the children of Leningrad after they had survived a winter of starvation. He wrote the following.

"(W)hen I first saw the Leningrad children . . . the hard experience of the winter was still imprinted on their faces and was still reflected in their games. (M)any of the children played all by themselves . . . even in their collective games, they played in silence, with grave faces. I saw the faces of children which expressed so grown-up a seriousness, children's eyes which expressed such thoughtfulness and sorrow, that those faces and eyes told one more than could be gathered from all the stories of the horrors of famine."

BENITO MUSSOLINI AND THE ITALIAN CAMPAIGNS

Throughout the war in Europe, Benito Mussolini, the fascist dictator of Italy, was both an important ally and a major annoyance to the Third Reich. Mussolini was loyal to Hitler, but he also dreamed of creating a new Roman empire.

From Italy's spot in the Mediterranean Sea, Mussolini looked to claim neighboring Yugoslavia, Albania, and Greece. He also planned to conquer the North Africa countries of Tunisia, Algeria, Libya, and Egypt.

The majority of Mussolini's military campaigns, however, were not successful. He did manage to take control of Albania, but his efforts in Yugoslavia, Greece, and Africa were disorganized and weak.

Map of Africa and the Mediterranean during World War II

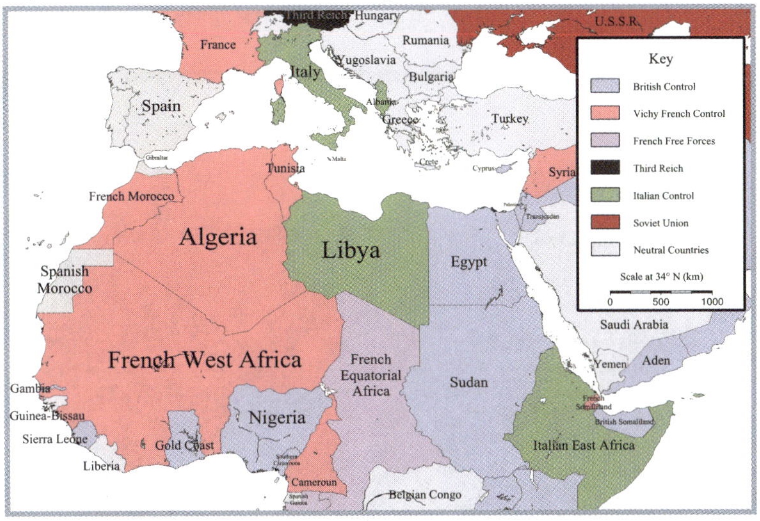

The success Mussolini had in Greece and Yugoslavia was largely due to German help. German forces in Africa tested the Allies far more than Italian forces did.

The country of Italy played an important role in Allied and Axis fighting in World War II. Late in the war especially, the country was divided between German forces in the north, and American and British forces in the south, struggling to open a road to France and Germany.

By then, however, Mussolini had lost control of his country. Even the Germans could not save the once-proud dictator from the partisans who eventually took his life.

DEATH SQUADS

We have already seen that German troops were willing to kill civilians as they invaded Western Europe. In Ukraine and Russia, however, civilian deaths intensified due to the efforts of an elite group of Nazi soldiers called the Einsatzgruppen.

NORTH AFRICAN CAMPAIGN

From June 1940 to May 1943, Allied and Axis forces fought for control of colonies and natural resources in North Africa. Fighting raged along a 3,000-mile front, from Morocco to Egypt, and resulted in 400,000 total casualties.

Africa was pulled into the conflict when Benito Mussolini declared war on Britain and France, the two largest colonial rulers in Africa. While Hitler battled to make Europe part of his Third Reich, Mussolini battled to claim African territories that had once belonged to the ancient Roman Empire.

When the United States entered World War II, Tunisia, Algeria, Libya, and Egypt were some of the first places where American troops faced off against both Italian and German armies. The Allies took the fight to Europe only after they had subdued North Africa.

New arrivals at Auschwitz-Birkenau, 1944, from a photo album found by a survivor and donated to Yad Vashem.

credit: Yad Vashem

The Einsatzgruppen were death squads. Their job was to murder Jews. After a town had been occupied by German troops, the Einsatzgruppen rounded up all the Jewish people they could find.

Mirgazim Sabirov survived the Einsatzgruppen at Babi Yar. Listen to his story here.

PS

Babi Yar Sabirov

They forced their victims to the edges of large, open graves, and shot them at close range, letting them drop dead into the gaping pits.

Sometimes, the death squads executed only a handful of Jews. Other times, as in the massacre at Babi Yar in Ukraine, they killed tens of thousands during the course of several days.

KILLING CENTERS OF THE HOLOCAUST

The Einsatzgruppen were ruthlessly efficient in their work. But even men trained to regard Jews as subhuman suffered mentally and emotionally under the strain of repeated mass executions. It was for this reason—the mental well-being of the Einsatzgruppen—that Nazi leader Heinrich Himmler first developed large-scale gassing operations.

The Nazis built many of these extermination camps in Poland, but the largest and deadliest was Auschwitz-Birkenau. It alone claimed the lives of more than 1 million people.

The manner of these deaths was horrifying in every detail. Jews from all over Europe were transported to killing centers in railroad cattle cars. Stuffed into small spaces with no food, no water, no toilet facilities, and not enough air to breathe, significant numbers of people died just making the trip.

> Those who survived were deposited directly from the train cars into the middle of the extermination camp and immediately sorted.

Men were separated from women and children. Those appearing strong enough to work were pulled aside to become forced laborers in the camp. Even those spared in the first winnowing, however, could not expect to live long. They survived on starvation rations, lived in filthy, overcrowded bunkhouses, and were worked beyond human endurance.

HELP FROM THE UNITED STATES

The United States did not officially enter World War II until the Japanese bombed Pearl Harbor in 1941. But it was never totally on the sidelines, and from the beginning, it was obvious where U.S. loyalty lay.

Early on, the United States assisted the Allies by protecting merchant convoys transporting goods from America to Great Britain across the Atlantic Ocean. Great Britain depended on those imports, and Germany had set up a submarine blockade to prevent them from getting in. The United States also assisted with a program called Lend-Lease. In this arrangement, the United States supplied vital resources—food, oil, warplanes, warships, and ammunition—at no cost upfront. In return, the Allies agreed to lease army and naval bases to the United States.

Everyone else was slated for death. They were led to what they were told was a communal shower. It was a clever ruse. After the filth of the long train ride, a shower seemed a welcome thing. Hundreds at a time, Jews filed naked into the death chambers. The doors locked behind them. Carbon monoxide gas or a poison gas called Zyklon B was released through fake shower heads. Within 30 minutes, everyone in the chamber had died of suffocation.

> The Nazis carried out the Holocaust—the extermination of 6 million Jews and millions more Slavs, Romani, and other targeted groups—in killing centers such as Auschwitz-Birkenau.

As the Nazi army spread death and destruction throughout Europe, tragic events were unfolding thousands of miles away in the Pacific Ocean. In the next chapter, we'll see how the Empire of Japan vastly expanded the scope of World War II.

BATTLE WATCH

In addition to the mass execution of Jews, the Nazis also targeted the Slavic peoples of Eastern Europe for extermination. They, too, were considered subhuman. Millions of Slavic noncombatants were killed.

Shoah **is the modern Hebrew word for holocaust.**

KEY QUESTIONS

- **How would you have handled the nightly bombings that the people of London experienced during the Battle of Britain?**
- **Why did the United States delay its entry into the war? How might the war and Holocaust have been different if the United States had been involved sooner?**
- **How might the Russian experience of World War II continue to shape Russian culture today?**

HOMETOWN INVASION AND RESISTANCE

In every war, there are people who are attacking and there are people who are defending. The strategies for each position are very different.

- **Divide your classmates or friends into two groups.** One group is going to plan an invasion of your hometown. The other is going to plan a resistance. Your missions are different, but your task is the same—to identify the strengths and weaknesses of your town.
- **Study a map of your town.**
  - What are the advantages or disadvantages of the terrain?
  - What are the major routes in or out of town? Are there airports, railroads, or bridges?
  - Are there any military facilities in the area?
  - How does your town provide basic necessities such as food, water, electricity, and heating fuel?
  - Are there any industries that might be subject to attack, or that can be used to assist the resistance?
  - Where is the seat of government located?
- **When each group has finished its research, get back together and share the results.**
  - What did the other side think of that you didn't?
  - What new things did you learn about where you live?

To investigate more, research the plans your town already has in place to respond to emergencies. What type of emergencies is your town prepared for? What emergencies have they responded to in the past? What agencies are responsible for emergency preparedness?

Inquire & Investigate

PREVENT STARVATION

Throughout World War II, especially in Europe and Russia, starvation was a constant concern. Labor and fuel shortages limited harvests and made it difficult to move food to markets. As a result, food was scarce and there was strict rationing. People frequently planted vegetable gardens, called victory gardens, in any available outdoor space. In European cities, where there was little space between and around buildings, people had to be creative.

- **Form a group with friends or classmates and take a walk around your neighborhood.** Your goal is to figure out where you can grow food.
  - How much land is available? Do homes have front or back yards? Are there parks or medians that you can use?
  - Is the available terrain easy to garden? Is it hilly or flat? Heavily or sparsely wooded? Do you have access to water?
  - Does the soil lend itself to gardening? How can you tell?
- **Draw up a map of where you will plant your gardens and indicate what you will grow.** Can you calculate how much food you will produce or how many people you will be able to feed?

To investigate more, find out as much as you can about where your food comes from right now. Is much of it grown locally or is it transported from far away? If the food distribution system in your area were disrupted, what products would stop showing up in the grocery store?

VOCAB LAB

Write down what you think each word means. What root words can you find to help you? What does the context of the word tell you?

Blitz, **civilian**, **evacuation**, **formidable**, **mobilize**, **occupation**, **resilient**, **resistance**, **siege**, and **warmonger**.

Compare your definitions with those of your friends or classmates. Did you all come up with the same meanings? Turn to the text and glossary if you need help.

Chapter 4

The Bombing of Pearl Harbor

Why did the United States enter World War II?

When Japan bombed Pearl Harbor in Hawaii, the United States realized it had to defend itself and the ideals of democracy from the threat of the Axis powers.

By December 1941, World War II had been raging for two years. Nazi Germany occupied most of Western Europe. The Luftwaffe had repeatedly bombed Great Britain. Germany had invaded Russia. Benito Mussolini's troops were in North Africa and Axis forces were in Greece and Yugoslavia. Where were the Americans?

The United States remained on the sidelines. Political leaders offered the Allies equipment and protection on the open ocean, but the country had not committed any soldiers to the fight.

On December 7, 1941, that changed. When Japanese warplanes bombed the American naval base at Pearl Harbor in Oahu, Hawaii, the United States became a major player in World War II.

A new theater of military operations opened up in the Pacific Ocean.

THE PATH TO PEARL HARBOR

Japan was a country of just 73 million people. The United States was a country of more than 130 million, and its industrial and military capabilities were far more robust than those of Japan. Many of Japan's leaders knew they could not win a full-scale war against the United States. So why attack?

To understand Japan's actions requires a long-term historical perspective. Its decisions in World War II were not made overnight. For hundreds of years, Japan had been an insulated country rooted in a feudal past. Prior to the nineteenth century, while Western nations made giant leaps forward in technological and military innovations, Japan fell behind.

In 1853, Japan was a peaceful nation, content in its isolation, when four American warships arrived in Tokyo Bay. They brought with them Commodore Matthew Perry (1794–1858), and he demanded U.S. access to Japanese islands.

Japan refused Perry's demands. But it was a useless act of defiance. Japan's military was so outdated, the country had no way of defending itself. In March 1854, Japan signed an agreement to open its ports to the United States.

JAPAN'S IMPERIAL AMBITIONS

Despite its outdated military, Japan was determined to remain strong and independent. Instead of giving in to American demands, the country reinvented itself. Starting in 1868, in an era known as the Meiji Restoration, Japan industrialized its economy and updated its military with remarkable speed. Within a few decades, Japan's economy and its armed forces were equal to those of Europe.

BATTLE WATCH

The Pacific Ocean is large enough to contain all of the landmasses on Earth—with room to spare. It is the largest physical feature on the planet.

The Sino-Japanese War

Japan's second invasion of China lasted from 1937 to 1945. It was the largest Asian conflict of the twentieth century, and also one of the most horrific. When the Japanese overran the Chinese capital of Nanking from December 13, 1937, to January 1938, Japanese soldiers tortured and murdered an estimated 300,000 people. This event is known as the Nanking Massacre, or the Rape of Nanking.

PS

Read three first-person accounts of the Rape of Nanking.

Nanking first person accounts

As the country grew stronger, Japan began to want to add to its territory. Japan's leaders saw how Western nations had grown richer and more powerful by colonizing other peoples. They decided to do the same.

Starting in 1895, Japan seized Taiwan from China. Japan also battled Russia over Chinese Manchuria and took over Korea. During World War I, Japan sided with the Allies, and was rewarded with some of Germany's Pacific islands.

But the ultimate prize for Japan was China, a potential source of tremendous wealth in natural resources and human capital. Japan viewed the Chinese people the same way that Great Britain viewed the people of India—as an inferior race that needed the rule of a superior civilization.

In 1931, Japan invaded Chinese Manchuria.

JAPANESE RELATIONS WITH THE WEST

Japanese leaders believed they were equal, if not superior, to their Western counterparts. So, when Japan invaded Manchuria, it expected support from its Western allies. To Japan's surprise, the Western nations reacted with alarm. They threatened sanctions if Japan did not pull back.

This confused the Japanese. European countries had expanded their empires through colonization for centuries. Why were they opposed to Japan's move to colonize China?

Japan moved ahead, invading China again in 1937. This time, the United States punished Japan by suspending its commercial treaty with the country.

Worse still, America, France, and Great Britain sent aid to China, the very country that Japan aimed to colonize. Japan felt even more betrayed by the Western powers after Germany invaded Poland in 1939.

In 1940, Japan invaded French Indochina, now known as Vietnam, hoping to halt the flow of aid to China and force the Chinese to surrender. The United States responded by sending 400 warplanes to the Philippines, which is only about 2,000 miles from Japan. Soon after, the United States, Britain, and the Netherlands stopped selling oil to Japan. Without oil, Japan's economy and military would be badly hurt.

Threatened by powerful outside forces, and with no access to the raw materials that their country needed, such as oil, Japan's leaders were in a bind. They would have to give up their military and imperial ambitions in order to resume trade relations with the Western powers.

Encouraged by Hitler's promise that Germany and Italy would go to war with the United States once Japan did, Japan prepared to fight back.

Once Japan's oil supplies were cut off, the country was in need of allies. So it joined up with Germany and Italy, becoming the third member of the Axis powers.

THE EMPEROR AND THE MILITARY

Japan in the 1930s and 1940s was one of the most militarized countries in the world. Every part of Japanese society was geared toward an idealization of military strength. Children, in particular, were immersed in a military culture. Every child received mandatory military training in school and was taught that there was no greater honor than to die in battle for Emperor Hirohito.

BATTLE WATCH

Hawaii did not become the 50th state until August 1959. At the time of the Japanese attack on Pearl Harbor, Hawaii was an incorporated territory of the United States.

On the surface, the young Emperor Hirohito was a supreme leader who ruled by divine right. His subjects viewed him as a god.

> They pledged their loyalty to him and considered him all-wise and all-powerful.

In reality, however, Emperor Hirohito rarely used his power. Military leaders controlled Japan, and Emperor Hirohito went along with them.

In late 1941, their orders were to attack Pearl Harbor. If they dealt a crushing blow to the U.S. Navy, Japan's leaders figured they stood a chance of seizing control of the European colonies in the Pacific. That would give them access to what they needed—a rich supply of oil.

A Personal Perspective

Donald Stratton (1922–), a Navy serviceman aboard the USS *Arizona*, describes his experiences of the attack on Pearl Harbor.

"Bombs were going off everywhere. Great billows of smoke were eating up the blue sky and turning it black. Torpedoes slammed against our hulls, spewing geysers of water into the air. Ships were taking on water. . . . And from those ruptured ships spilled oil that congealed when it hit the water and caught fire . . . .

One explosion followed another, and after each one you could hear twisted metal writhing. . . . Machine gun bullets ricocheted off metal. . . . And the fury of our own antiaircraft guns, reverberating inside our metal cubicle so loudly I thought my eardrums were going to burst."[1]

ATTACK ON PEARL HARBOR

Few people were prepared for what happened on the morning of December 7, 1941. Relations were strained between the United States and Japan, and U.S. intelligence sources had picked up some hints that Japan might be planning an attack. But if the Japanese did strike, the United States assumed they would target the Philippines, not Hawaii.

Pearl Harbor was not under high alert. The base's guns were unmanned. Stores of ammunitions were locked up. Aircraft were parked in the open, lined up wingtip to wingtip, making them easy targets.

Most people at Pearl Harbor were asleep when hundreds of Japanese warplanes, under the command of Admiral Isoroku Yamamoto (1884–1943), first roared into sight. People staggered from their beds, dressing on the run, as bombs exploded all around them.

The Americans responded as best they could. They fired back with antiaircraft guns and launched a handful of warships. But they had been caught off guard, and their efforts to defend themselves were largely ineffective.

The attack on Pearl Harbor lasted just 90 minutes, but it killed more than 2,400 U.S. military personnel and wounded nearly 1,200 more. There was a great loss of ships and airplanes. The Japanese sank 18 U.S. ships, destroyed 188 aircraft, and damaged another 159.

Japanese forces lost just 29 planes and suffered damage to only 74. Pearl Harbor cost the Japanese 64 lives.

Listen to more stories and view photographs of Pearl Harbor.

PS

Pearl Harbor eyewitness accounts youtube

The bombing of Pearl Harbor

credit: National Archives

AMERICA RESPONDS

On December 8, President Roosevelt stood before a joint session of the U.S. House of Representatives and Senate. Referring to the attack as a "date which will live in infamy," President Roosevelt asked for a declaration of war. The measure passed almost unanimously. Only one member, Rep. Jeanette Rankin (1880–1973), of Montana, voted against it.

> As promised, Germany and Italy and their allies, Hungary, Romania, and Bulgaria, immediately declared war on the United States.

Within days, hundreds of thousands of American men lined up outside military recruitment offices, eager to enlist. In some places, recruitment offices stayed open 24 hours a day, seven days a week, trying to accommodate the rush of volunteers.

Officials turned away veterans of World War I because they were too old to serve, but they let slide through teenagers who had not yet turned 18 but were determined to enlist. Between enlistments and draftees, the U.S. military during World War II had a force of around 16 million people.

Signing up was easy. Becoming a soldier was not. New recruits were given just six weeks of basic training—down from 12 weeks that was the norm during peacetime. Basic training was followed by weeks, or even months, of specialty training in areas such as intelligence, engineering, or transportation. Only then were soldiers loaded onto huge troop ships and carried overseas to do battle.

BATTLE WATCH

Naval officer Kazuo Sakamaki (1918–1999) was captured by Americans during the attack on Pearl Harbor. He became the first Japanese prisoner of war in World War II.

A Marine recruitment poster targeting women

credit: National Archives

THE ROLE OF MINORITIES

In 1941, all branches of the U.S. armed services were segregated—blacks and whites couldn't serve alongside each other. Still, millions of African American men volunteered to serve their country.

At first, they worked almost exclusively as truck drivers and dock workers. By 1944, however, African American members of the 99th Fighter Squadron, also known as the Tuskegee Airmen, gained fame and medals for their courage and abilities in the air.

That same year, black troops fought next to their white counterparts on the ground in the Battle of the Bulge in France and Belgium.

American women, both black and white, came forward to serve their country, too. Although barred from direct combat roles, they filled other vital positions. About 74,000 women became Army and Navy nurses. More than 150,000 women signed up for the Women's Army Corps (WAC). Others joined the Marine Corps Women's Reserve, the Navy Women's Reserve, and the Coast Guard. Altogether, about 350,000 women served in the military during World War II.

CONCENTRATION CAMPS IN AMERICA

The willingness of men and women to defend their country was a positive side of American patriotism. Unfortunately, America's response to Pearl Harbor also revealed a dark side.

NISEI TROOPS

More than 30,000 native-born Japanese Americans, or Nisei, served in the U.S. armed forces in World War II. They worked in segregated units under the command of white officers and most were deployed to war zones in Europe. The 442nd Regimental Combat Team, a Nisei unit, became one of the most decorated forces in U.S. military history. The Medal of Honor, the highest recognition for valor, was given to Sadao Munemori (1922–1945), who died in Italy while protecting the lives of his fellow soldiers.

A Personal Perspective

Richard Karasawa (1928–) was 14 years old when he and his family were relocated to the Santa Anita racetrack in California. He described their housing in former horse stables.

"The horse urine was so strong you could never get rid of that smell. So when I'd visit my friends, I couldn't stay there long because of the horse urine. I don't know how they could stand it . . . and I'm from a farm family, I was around horses all the time you know."[2]

Within three months after Pearl Harbor, President Roosevelt signed an executive order that required many Japanese Americans to be relocated to government-controlled concentration camps. People affected by this order lived in California and Nevada, and in the western counties of Washington, Oregon, and Arizona.

They were forced out of their homes and loaded onto buses and trains that took them to camps located as far away as Tennessee, Colorado, Arkansas, Idaho, and Texas.

The first stops, however, were temporary relocation centers. These were hastily assembled camps set up at horse racing tracks, warehouses, and county fairgrounds. Conditions were horrific. The camps were enclosed with barbed wire and patrolled by military police wielding machine guns. Families were lodged in converted horse stables or warehouses.

The Minidoka War Relocation Authority Center, 1942

credit: Francis Stewart, National Archives

Why did the U.S. government order so many people of Japanese descent to be kept in internment camps? Political leaders said that these people were possible threats to U.S. security.

Today, it's understood that more than 130,000 innocent people were held because of racism, not national safety. In 1988, the U.S. government acknowledged the injustice that had been done to Japanese Americans during World War II.

President Ronald Reagan (1911–2004) issued a formal apology and signed a bill that provided reparations in the amount of $20,000 for each individual harmed by being held in an internment camp.

In the next two chapters, we'll see how the United States worked with the Allies to change the course of World War II. Through all the stories of heroism and sacrifice, however, we must never forget how the United States wrongfully imprisoned its Japanese citizens. We must honor our fallen soldiers without justifying that shame.

OTHER ETHNIC INTERNEES

The United States was not at war only with Japan. It was also at war with Italy and Germany. As a result, some Italian and German citizens were imprisoned as possible enemies of the country. Their numbers, however, never got close to those of their Japanese-American counterparts. It would have been impossible to arrest and detain the millions of Americans of Italian and German descent. And that plan might have discouraged many European immigrants from joining the U.S. armed forces.

KEY QUESTIONS

- **How might World War II have played out if Japan hadn't attacked the United States?**
- **Was it fair that Western powers disapproved of Japan's invasion of China? Why or why not?**
- **What role did racism play in the U.S. response to the bombing of Pearl Harbor?**

Explore more narratives from Japanese Americans interned during World War II.

PS

Telling stories internment

Inquire & Investigate

THE PRESIDENT SPEAKS

On December 8, 1941, Americans tuned their radios to hear President Roosevelt call on Congress to declare war against Japan. You can listen to that address at this website. In an era before television, this is most likely how you would have experienced this historic event.

Roosevelt Congress war

- **Discuss your reaction to President Roosevelt's speech among your classmates or friends, or write a journal entry.**
  - What is the emotional and political atmosphere surrounding this speech?
  - Did you learn anything new by listening to this broadcast?
  - What is your impression of President Roosevelt?
- **Would you have chosen to take the United States to war?** Or would you have followed the lead of Rep. Jeanette Rankin, who voted against the war? Compose and deliver a brief speech of your own, outlining your reasons for either going to war or staying out of the fight. Assume your audience is made up of friends or classmates.

To investigate more, visit the website below and listen to or watch speeches that other presidents of the United States have given. Compare and contrast one of those speeches with the one you listened to from President Roosevelt. How do they differ in style, language, and substance? How are they similar?

Miller Center presidential speeches

THE PACIFIST

Jeanette Rankin was the first woman elected to the U.S. House of Representatives. She was also a pacifist. She believed conflicts must be resolved through diplomacy rather than through war. As a result, she voted against the United States taking up arms against Japan. Many people accused Rep. Rankin of disloyalty. Others threatened her with physical harm. But she refused to back down from her beliefs. In 1968, at age 87, she campaigned against U.S. involvement in the Vietnam War.

CONSCIENTIOUS OBJECTORS

Conscientious objectors (COs) are people who, for moral or religious reasons, refuse to take up arms during times of war. During World War I, COs were treated as criminals. In World War II, however, they were allowed to serve their country in other ways.

- **Read more about them and explore their stories at these websites.**
  - Why did people become COs?
  - How did they support the war effort without fighting?
  - Do you think the country supported their decision to refrain from combat?

Nebraska conscientious

Swarthmore conscientious

civilian conscientious

- **Create a presentation about one CO and share your findings with classmates or friends.** What did you learn about COs that surprised you? Do you think they made the right decision? Do you consider them patriots?

To investigate more, read two poems by American poet Edna St. Vincent Millay (1892–1950), "Conscientious Objector" and "Poem and Prayer for an Invading Army." In 1934, when "Conscientious Objector" was published, Millay was an avowed pacifist. By 1944, when she published "Poem and Prayer for an Invading Army," her views had changed. Why do you think that happened? What about World War II could have caused Millay to support armed conflict?

Inquire & Investigate

VOCAB LAB

Write down what you think each word means. What root words can you find to help you? What does the context of the word tell you?

colonize, **feudal**, **immigrant**, **imperial**, **internment camp**, **Nisei**, **pacifist**, and **segregate**.

Compare your definitions with those of your friends or classmates. Did you all come up with the same meanings? Turn to the text and glossary if you need help.

Inquire & Investigate

YOU'RE IN THE ARMY NOW!

When you join an army, you need to quickly memorize the insignia, or badges, and ranks of your fellow service members. These links show some of the insignia worn in the U.S. Army.

Enlisted men and women	WWII badges
Officers	WWII badges officers

- **Use art materials to make your own badges.**
  - What shapes symbolize your country or region?
  - What colors indicate your military goals or rank?
  - Do you include any words on your badge?
- **Have your friends or classmates design their own badges.** It's important to know what different badges mean in the armed forces. Can you memorize your friends' badges so you know immediately what they mean?

To investigate more, explore the five different branches of the U.S. armed forces: Air Force, Army, Marine Corps, Coast Guard, and Navy. If you had enlisted or been drafted during World War II, which branch of the armed forces would you have wanted to join?

Chapter 5

War in the Pacific and Asia

What challenges did soldiers face when fighting in the Pacific?

An unforgiving landscape and a lack of supplies and experience made it extremely difficult for the Allied soldiers in the Pacific theater of war.

On December 7, 1941, Pearl Harbor was not the only place under fire by the Japanese. Six additional locations came under attack. Four were U.S. targets: the heavily populated Philippines and Guam, plus two sparsely populated coral islands called Wake Island and Midway Island, which housed U.S. naval and marine bases. That same day, Japan also invaded the British colonies of Malaya (Malaysia) and Hong Kong.

It was a shocking display of aggression, and a hint of things to come.

By early 1942, Japan gained control of Singapore and Burma. In June, they occupied Attu and Kiska, in the Aleutian Islands of Alaska. They were encroaching on the subcontinent of India and threatening northern Australia.

FIRST DAYS OF WAR IN THE PACIFIC

Japan had caught the Allies off guard. For two years, the Allies had focused their attention on battles in Europe and Africa. When war suddenly spread to the Pacific, they were too ill equipped and understaffed to respond effectively. As Hitler had done in Western Europe, Emperor Hirohito did in the Pacific. He won many crucial early battles.

To dominate Asia, Japan needed to control Manila Bay, a key commercial and military port located near the Philippines island of Luzon. In December 1941, American General Douglas MacArthur (1880–1964) was stationed in Manila.

BATTLE WATCH

The United States purchased Alaska from the Russian Empire in 1867, but Alaska was not officially admitted to the union until January 3, 1959.

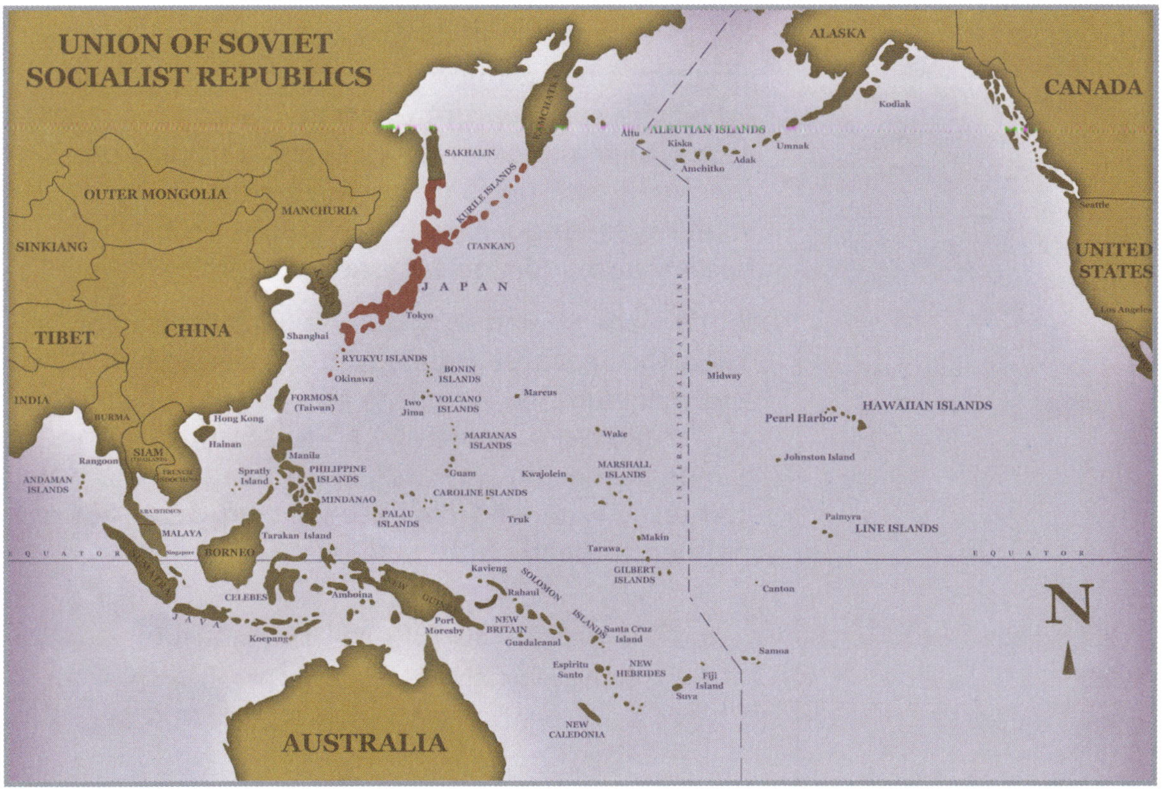

MacArthur had a total of 130,000 American and Filipino troops under his command, but the vast majority of them were untested in battle. When Japan invaded Luzon with 43,000 experienced soldiers, MacArthur was forced to retreat.

He led more than 100,000 soldiers and civilians into the Bataan Peninsula, located just to the west of Manila Bay. Trapped in harrowing conditions, without food or medicine, many people became malnourished and fell ill with malaria, dengue fever, and dysentery.

THE PHILIPPINES

The Philippines is a collection of more than 7,000 islands. Colonized by Spain in 1521, it became a territory of the United States in 1898 at the end of the Spanish-American War. By 1916, however, the United States was taking steps to grant independence to the Philippines. In 1935, it became a partially autonomous commonwealth, which meant it was somewhat self-governing, and in 1946, it gained full independence.

THE BATAAN DEATH MARCH

General MacArthur escaped Bataan unharmed when President Roosevelt had him evacuated to Australia in March 1942. From there, MacArthur famously proclaimed, "I shall return."

That was small comfort to the troops left behind under the command of General Edward King (1884–1958). Their situation was hopeless. Cut off from the world with no food, reinforcements, or medical supplies, three-quarters of the troops on Bataan became too ill or too famished to fight.

When General King surrendered Bataan on April 9, 1942, the Japanese ordered 76,000 desperately sick and malnourished American and Filipino prisoners of war (POWs) to march 60 miles north to POW camps. Along the way, they were denied food, water, and rest. Those who couldn't keep up were shot or stabbed to death with bayonets.

This forced removal came to be known as the Bataan Death March.

Prisoners on the Bataan Death March

credit: National Archives

Trudging over rugged terrain in sweltering heat, men dropped from dehydration and exhaustion. Even after POWs reached the camps, they continued to die by the hundreds every day.

Corporal Glenn Frazier (1923–) was a U.S. soldier stationed in Manila. He survived the Bataan Death March, which he describes here.

> "When a guy was bayoneted or shot, lying in the road, and the convoys were coming along, I saw trucks . . . go out of their way to run over the guy in the middle of the road. . . . And I saw men beaten with a rifle butt until there was just no more life in them. I saw Filipino women [who tried to bring us food or water] cut. Their stomachs were cut open. Their throats were cut. I saw Filipinos and Americans beheaded just with one swipe of a saber."[1]

Nurse POWs

At the outset of conflict in the Pacific, 78 nurses from the U.S. Army and Navy were stationed at hospitals in the Philippines. Captured by the Japanese, they were held as prisoners of war from 1941 to 1945. They continued to provide nursing services when they could, but they suffered many of the same deprivations as male POWs. Nicknamed the "Battling Belles of Bataan," they were awarded the Bronze Star for valor and the Presidential Unit Citation for heroism in action.

THE ISLAND CAMPAIGNS

The United States is separated from Japan by more than 3,000 miles of the Pacific Ocean. As a result, one of the biggest challenges the United States faced in its war against Japan was the simple problem of how to get there. They had to find a way for ships and planes from Pearl Harbor to arrive on the Japanese mainland without running out of fuel along the way.

To solve that problem, Admiral Chester Nimitz (1885–1966) and General MacArthur were put in charge of a strategy called "island hopping." Japan, like the Philippines, is a collection of thousands of islands, most of which are quite small.

To approach Japan, Nimitz opened a route across the Central Pacific by taking over one small island at a time, almost like stepping stones in a garden.

A photographic flyover mission over Iwo Jima

credit: National Archives

Meanwhile, MacArthur approached through New Guinea and the South Pacific. Along the way, the captured smaller islands served as refueling and resupply stations, with airfields from which the United States could launch airstrikes against Japan.

Fighting conditions on the Pacific islands were of two distinctly different types. Many were dense, dark jungles, such as Guadalcanal, where tropical diseases sometimes put more soldiers out of commission than enemy fire. Others were volcanic islands, such as Iwo Jima, with virtually no vegetation to break up an alien landscape of gray rock and black sand.

Underneath the desolate surface of the volcanic islands, the Japanese constructed many miles of interconnected tunnels and caves. These formed a nightmarish subterranean stronghold from which Japanese soldiers desperately fought to prevent U.S. forces from reaching mainland Japan.

DEATH BEFORE DISHONOR

All the island battles shared one striking similarity. The Japanese fought with a fanaticism that U.S. troops found difficult to comprehend and that was terrifying to witness. It's an exaggeration to say that Japanese soldiers never surrendered. They sometimes did, but not often.

For example, when fighting started on Iwo Jima, more than 20,000 Japanese servicemen defended the island. When the fighting ended, only 216 were captured alive. Many who had not been killed by enemy fire chose ritual suicide over surrender.

In other battles, such as at Okinawa, U.S. servicemen combated fearless Japanese pilots known as the kamikaze.

BRAINWASHING

Japanese military training involved brainwashing for the purpose of breaking men's wills. New recruits were severely beaten by their superior officers. They were verbally abused, belittled, and repeatedly made to believe that their enemies were subhuman. They were required to execute prisoners by severing men's heads from their bodies with one blow of a sword. They practiced bayonet charges on live human beings. Said Shozo Tominaga (1914–2002), a lieutenant in the Imperial Japanese Army, "After that, a man could do anything easily."[2]

In Japanese, *kamikaze* means "divine wind." In the battle of Okinawa, kamikaze attacks inflicted more damage on the U.S. Navy than in any other single battle in U.S. naval history.

These elite pilots loaded warplanes with bombs and fuel tanks and flew them into enemy ships, knowing they would die in the explosion. To the U.S. troops, it seemed an insane thing to do, but there was logic behind the apparent madness.

If the United States captured Okinawa, the path to mainland Japan would be clear. More than 3,800 kamikaze pilots chose to die rather than let that happen.

The Japanese Home Front

Japanese civilians confronted many of the same challenges as did noncombatants in Europe. They endured bomb raids that destroyed homes and lives, and they sent their children into the countryside to protect them. Food was strictly rationed, so they got creative in finding ways to grow food of their own.

With millions of men funneled into military service, Japanese women went to work in industries that supported the war effort. In normal times, a female machinist or truck driver would have caused a scandal in the conservative, traditional society of Japan. For a while, the necessities of war loosened those cultural constraints. But as happened elsewhere, when the war ended, Japanese women were relegated to the home once again.

AIR RAIDS OVER JAPAN

By June 1944, the United States was finally in a position to fly air raids over Japan. These missions were carried out in two ways—precision bombing and fire bombing.

The air raid campaigns started with precision bombing. These missions dropped bombs on specific targets, such as weapons factories, oil depots, airports, and bridges. They used conventional bombs that caused damage by the force of an explosion.

Starting in March 1945, the United States switched to a strategy of fire bombing. Bombs were outfitted with incendiary devices and dropped over heavily populated areas. Specific targets were destroyed by burning down the cities around them. In Japan, where many houses were constructed of paper and wood, fire bombs caused massive destruction.

In a typical attack, 200 to 300 warplanes appeared in the night sky and released thousands of tons of fire bombs on the civilian population below. Deaths and injuries from a single attack numbered in the tens of thousands. Even more people were left homeless. In Tokyo alone, an estimated 1 million people lost their homes.

THE FORGOTTEN WAR

For most of World War II, the public focused its gaze on events in Europe, Africa, and the Pacific. But fearsome battles were also fought in China, Burma, and India. Collectively, they were called the CBI theater of operations.

CBI received so little attention that many people referred to it as the Forgotten War, but the CBI battles were critically important for the countries involved.

BATTLE WATCH

The United States bombed more than 60 Japanese cities. During the war, most Americans approved of targeting civilian populations in both Germany and Japan. After the war, however, more people began to question the morality of such actions.

Tokyo after being fire bombed, 1945

credit: Fukao Kōzō

When you look at a map of Asia, you can see how Burma, now called Myanmar, sits like a wedge between western China and northeast India. That's where most of the fighting in the CBI campaigns took place.

BATTLE WATCH

In March 1944, Japan invaded India when troops besieged the city of Imphal. Allied troops forced them back out in July of the same year.

Japanese forces were pushing to invade India through Burma. Allied forces were pushing them back.

Every war environment presents its own challenges. In the CBI campaigns, deep in the jungles of Burma, men climbed mountains that were thousands of feet high. Sometimes, the slopes were so steep, soldiers crawled on all fours, grabbing at tree roots to avoid slipping backwards.

> During rainy seasons, troops slogged through mud 2 feet deep and as thick as oatmeal.

Map of Burma, India, and China

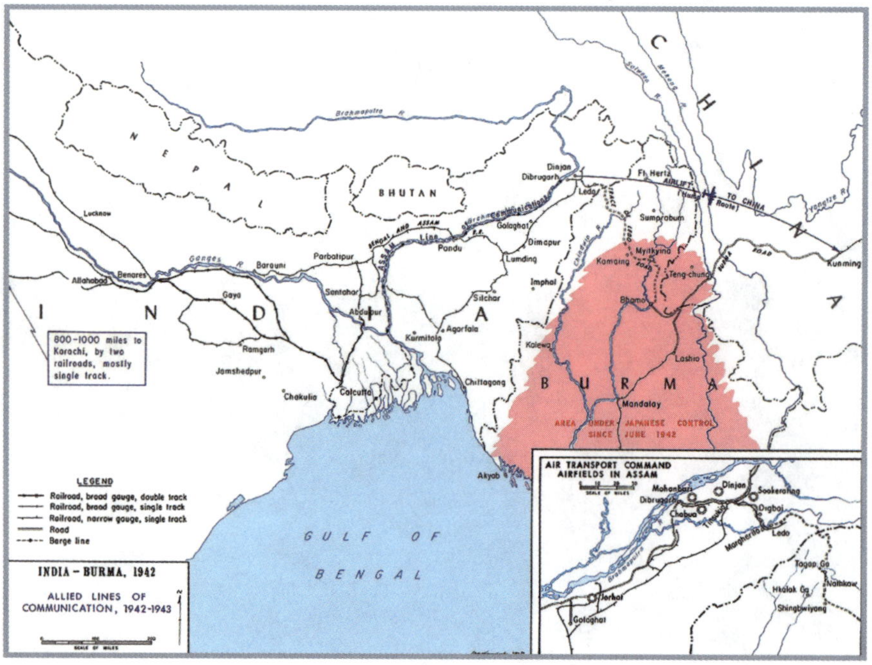

Leeches were another problem. They attached themselves to men's bodies and filled up on blood until they ballooned in size. If not properly removed, the leeches' heads remained stuck under the skin and caused serious infections. The men learned to remove them with the tips of lit cigarettes.

FLYING THE HUMP AND THE BURMA ROAD

Allied forces in the CBI theater had the job of keeping Japan out of India while also keeping supplies coming into China. Japan had cut off China's access to supplies by sea, so the only way to keep China supplied was to send goods by road out of India and through Burma or to send them by airplane over the Himalayan Mountains.

Neither route was easy. The Himalayas are some of the tallest mountains in the world. To fly over them with the flight technology available in the 1940s required pilots of considerable daring and skill. They called the mission "flying the hump." Pilots might take off in steamy jungle conditions only to find themselves flying to an altitude where the temperatures dipped below freezing.

They flew more than 500 miles each way through storms and fog and enemy fire.

Tougher still was the reopening of the route through Burma on the Burma Road, the main overland supply route from India to China. Even under ideal conditions, engineering a road through dense jungles, deep rivers, and soaring mountains was a monumental undertaking. To do so while under attack by the Japanese army was even harder.

Burma Road

credit: National Archives

The job got done under the command of an American general named Joseph Stilwell (1883–1946). He was a short-tempered man whom his troops nicknamed "Vinegar Joe." General Stilwell led an international force made up of American, British, Indian, Nepalese, and Chinese personnel who created a 1,100-mile highway that linked up with the Burma Road.

To complete the job required enormous hardship and sacrifice. The men laid a mile of road a day, but at the cost of one American soldier per mile. Some were killed or injured by Japanese snipers. Fourteen times more people, however, were evacuated due to disease and accidents.

After the bombing of Pearl Harbor, America sent its first soldiers of World War II into the Pacific and to Asia with little support or input from the other Allied nations. The final outcome of the war, however, hinged on the ability of four powerful countries to work together toward a common goal.

The next chapter explores how Great Britain, Russia, China, and the United States formulated and carried out a plan for victory.

VOCAB LAB

Write down what you think each word means. What root words can you find to help you? What does the context of the word tell you?

brainwash, **fanaticism**, **fire bombing**, **kamikaze**, **morality**, **peninsula**, **fanaticism**, **sniper**, **subhuman**, and **subterranean**.

Compare your definitions with those of your friends or classmates. Did you all come up with the same meanings? Turn to the text and glossary if you need help.

KEY QUESTIONS

- **Why weren't the Allied powers better prepared for war after the Japanese bombed Pearl Harbor?**
- **What were some of the hardships that Allied and Axis troops faced in the Pacific island battles?**
- **Why were the China-Burma-India campaigns referred to as the "forgotten war"?**

TOUR THE PACIFIC ISLANDS AND ASIA

Battles in the Pacific and Asia turned some of the most beautiful and exotic places on Earth into landscapes of nightmares. What are these places like today? Did the war have lingering effects on the geography or cultures there?

- **Using tourism and travel guides online or from the library, plan a trip to one of the following countries.**
    - The Philippines
    - Malaysia
    - Japan
    - China
    - Indonesia
    - Australia
    - India
- **Make your visit as long as you like, and visit whatever cities and tourist destinations you want.**
    - Which country did you choose and why?
    - Which cities do you want to visit?
    - What attractions do you want to see or experience? Are you interested in museums, outdoor adventures, theater, art, music, shopping?
- **Write a travel diary entry for each day of your trip.** You can also create a presentation that shows the places you visited and what you did.

To investigate more, do an online news search about the country you visited. What issues are being reported on today? Do any of today's news stories have connections to the events of World War II?

Inquire & Investigate

PACIFIC ISLAND WAR STORIES

There are many stories about World War II battles in the Pacific. You can find them in books, documentaries, and fictionalized historical movies.

- **Look for information online or in a book or movie about one of the battles in the Pacific.** Choose Pearl Harbor, Wake Island, Doolittle Raid, Midway Island, Guadalcanal, Marshall Islands, Guam, Leyte Gulf, Iwo Jima, or Okinawa.
- **Create a presentation that includes the following.**
  - A map that shows where the battle took place
  - Start and end dates of the battle
  - Number of casualties on both sides
  - A brief explanation of why the battle was significant
- **Consider the battle you chose in the context of the entire war.** Would the outcome of the war have been different if that battle never happened? How does it compare to other battles in terms of direct and indirect loss of life?

To investigate more, look up information about a memorial that has been created to commemorate the battle you researched. Where is the memorial located? When was it installed? What is it like?

Chapter 6
War's End

How does the world end a huge conflict being fought in several different regions?

It took a major amount of strategic planning and manpower on the part of the Allies to plan and execute a series of events that would finally win the war and bring peace.

Three years into the war, fighting continued in Russia, Africa, Italy, China, Burma, India, Japan, and the Pacific islands. Food shortages pushed civilians to the brink of starvation, even as they labored day and night in war industries. Jews throughout Europe faced death in concentration camps and killing centers. The Allied leaders—Roosevelt, Churchill, and Stalin—looked upon a world where the lives of millions of men, women, and children were in danger. Their job was to save these people.

After successfully leading the Allied invasion of French North Africa in late 1942 and 1943, General Dwight D. Eisenhower (1890–1969) of the United States was appointed supreme commander of the Allied forces. In 1953, Eisenhower would become the 34th president. In 1943, his job was to coordinate the Allied armies of Western Europe. Joseph Stalin coordinated the Allied armies in the East.

One of Eisenhower's biggest challenges was to determine how to distribute valuable resources. Allied leaders advocated for whatever seemed best for their individual countries. Military leaders, with strong opinions about how to conduct a war, asked for whatever troops and equipment they thought were needed to win.

It was impossible for Eisenhower to please everyone. Each country's situation was unique, and resources were limited. There were never enough troops, fuel, tanks, airplanes, guns, and ammunition to satisfy all those demands.

THE PLAN IN EUROPE

With Eisenhower in charge of the Western Front and Stalin in charge of the Eastern Front, the Allies mapped out a plan of attack. The first objective was to defeat the Axis forces that remained in North Africa. The idea was to succeed in Africa and then defeat the Germans with this plan.

- Drive Axis forces out of Sicily, located in the southwest of Italy.
- Use Sicily as a base to send Allied troops into the rest of Italy.
- Take control of Fascist Italy and push German troops north toward Central Europe.
- Stage an Allied invasion into German-occupied France.
- Continue attacking Axis troops in Southern and Western Europe.
- Bring Russian forces further west, across Poland, and into Germany.

EISENHOWER IN WORLD WAR I

General Dwight D. Eisenhower was the supreme commander of Allied forces in Western Europe during World War II. But he had never experienced military action in war. Eisenhower repeatedly asked to serve overseas in World War I, but he always received domestic assignments.

If things went as planned, Allied forces would converge on Germany from the west, the south, and the east all at the same time. The Nazi army would be defeated.

BATTLE WATCH

Malta, a small country south of Sicily, was an important, strategic spot, and whoever controlled it was likely to control the outcome of the war in Africa. The Allies were able to hold Malta during the entire war, but Malta was one of the most heavily bombed areas of World War II.

THE AFRICA CAMPAIGN

From our vantage point of the present, we know that the Allies' plans were successful. Victory, however, was never a foregone conclusion. Everywhere they fought, the Allies faced daunting challenges.

In North Africa, the war zone stretched nearly 3,000 miles, from Morocco in the west to Egypt in the east. Desert conditions brought scorching hot days, freezing nights, sandstorms, crippling thirst, and millions of flies. Attracted to the slightest hint of moisture, flies swarmed over men's faces, their sweaty clothes, and their food.

Map of the Mediterranean and Malta

credit: Central Intelligence Agency

U.S. troops in Northern Africa, 1942

credit: U.S. Army

Keeping supply routes open was another problem in Africa. Goods needed to be shipped in from the Mediterranean Sea, where warships and convoys were frequently under attack. Allied and Axis forces competed to see which side could sink the most enemy ships.

Whoever did was likely to control the African continent.

On the ground in Africa, the Allies squared off against one of Germany's most effective field marshals—Erwin Rommel (1891–1944). His successes in the early European campaigns had made Rommel one of Hitler's most trusted leaders. He proved his worth in Africa, too. Field Marshal Rommel landed in Libya with his "Afrika Korps" in February 1941 and kept the Allies at bay until May 1943.

WHAT'S IN A NAME?

Many generals emerged from World War II with nicknames that stuck with them long after the war ended.

People knew General Dwight D. Eisenhower as "Ike," British Field Marshal Bernard Montgomery (1887–1976) as "Monty," and Germany's Erwin Rommel as the "Desert Fox."

Those were the complimentary nicknames. Others were less flattering. Some people called General Douglas MacArthur "Dugout Doug" for the time he spent in underground bunkers while his troops suffered aboveground in the Philippines. General George Patton's (1885–1945) love of battle earned him the title "Old Blood and Guts."

THE ITALIAN CAMPAIGN

Prime Minister Winston Churchill had pushed hard for the Allies' next move to be the invasion of Italy. He often referred to Italy as the "soft underbelly" of Europe, insisting that Allied troops could easily "cut through" Italy and move on to Germany.

> Churchill got his way, but fighting in Italy proved far more difficult than anyone had imagined.

Everything went according to plan when the Allies took back control of Sicily in mid-August 1943, and the king of Italy, Vittorio Emanuele II (1820–1878), agreed to an armistice soon after. Now, the Italians were working with the Allies rather than against them.

Germany, however, fought back with a vengeance. Nazi troops flooded Italy from the north and fought the Allies, who were struggling to advance from the southern end of the country. Some of the most bitter and costly fighting took place in Italy. The battle of Monte Cassino alone took several months and four assaults before the Allies succeeded—at a cost of about 55,000 Allied casualties.

German soldiers also treated the Italian people brutally because they regarded them as traitors to the Nazi cause. For example, in 1944, in the village of Marzabotto, Nazi troops executed 770 Italian citizens who were accused of working with the resistance. Of these, 155 were children under the age of 10.

Fighting persisted in Italy until a few days before Germany surrendered in April 1945.

THE DOWNFALL OF MUSSOLINI

With the Allies gathering at his front door in the summer of 1943, Mussolini lost control of his government. King Vittorio Emanuele II imprisoned Mussolini for two months before he was rescued by German forces. For the next year and a half, Mussolini led a revived but ineffectual fascist government, until he was captured by partisans and shot to death.

BATTLE WATCH

In war, deaths and casualties are not the same thing. Deaths count people who have died. Casualties include the total number of military personnel wounded, killed, or missing in action.

THE NORMANDY INVASION

Of all the campaigns in Western Europe, none were more important than the Allied invasion of Nazi-occupied France. It was the largest seaborne invasion ever carried out in the world and a crucial turning point in the Second World War.

For years, Hitler's strategists had assumed the Allies would eventually strike back at Germany by coming through France. With Britain the only Western European country not neutral or under Nazi control, Germany also predicted that the Allies would prepare for the invasion in Britain. They kept a watchful eye on the English Channel, waiting for Allied ships to appear on the horizon.

Both sides prepared for the invasion. Beginning in June 1943, the British and Americans began the Combined Bomber Offensive, bombing German transport and industry targets. The Americans flew missions during the day while the British took over at night in an effort to destroy the Luftwaffe and Germany's ability to repel an invasion.

Hitler pulled Field Marshal Rommel out of Africa and assigned him to reinforce defensive positions all along the Atlantic coast into the North Sea, from southern France to the Netherlands and Denmark. Rommel lined the coast with mines, wooden stakes, metal tripods, barbed wire, and booby traps. Anything to interrupt the approach of troops and equipment coming ashore.

The beaches were also lined with thousands of pillboxes, small concrete fortifications from which German troops could fire at incoming enemies.

ITALY'S JEWS

Compared to Jews in other European countries, many Italian Jews managed to escape the full horror of the Holocaust. An Italian census of 1938 listed 45,000 Jews in the country. Of that number, 8,000 died in Nazi camps. Another 7,000 fled the country, and 30,000 lived in hiding until the end of the war.[1]

Pillboxes got their name because they resembled the cylindrical and hexagonal boxes that pills used to come in.

Normandy is an area of northern France. The name can be traced to the Danish and Norwegian Vikings, or Northmen, who settled the region in the ninth century.

On the other side of the English Channel, General Eisenhower assembled millions of Allied troops in England. He oversaw the development of special equipment to help with landing along the Normandy coast. The Allies also went to great lengths to deceive the Germans about when and where the invasion would take place.

To draw attention away from Normandy, Operation Fortitude convinced the Germans that the invasion would come in the Calais area on the coast of France, as well as from Norway. The Allies flooded the airwaves with fake reports of troop landings. They built dummy tanks and trucks and set them up near the coast.

They even kept one of their most capable generals, George Patton, stationed and inactive for weeks in Kent, England. That led the Germans to believe that the Allies intended to make two major offensives from the north, when, in fact, they planned only one.

D-DAY: JUNE 6, 1944

BATTLE WATCH

In military terminology, "D-Day" refers to the start of any major offensive. But for World War II, D-Day nearly always refers to the landing of Allied troops in Normandy.

The battlefield along the Normandy coast covered 50 miles of shoreline that was divided into five points of attack. From west to east, the key beaches were named Utah, Omaha, Gold, Juno, and Sword. On June 6, 1944, more than 150,000 Allied troops landed on the beaches.

U.S. troops landed mainly on Utah and Omaha. British troops were concentrated on Gold and Sword. Canadian troops were sent to Juno. Other countries were represented as well, including Poland, Norway, the Netherlands, and France.

The fighting on D-Day was some of the deadliest of the war.

American troops landing on the shores of Normandy

credit: U.S. Navy

Allied troops landing on the beaches were easy targets for German soldiers firing at them from pillboxes. Men, landing crafts, and tanks became ensnared in the impediments set up on the shore.

Mines exploded, shells rained down from warplanes overhead, and soldiers fought in hand-to-hand combat on the ground. The cost in lives was high on both sides. Historians debate the exact figures, but Allied casualties numbered at least 10,000, including 4,000 deaths. From their defensive positions on the beaches, German casualties were lower, but they were still in the thousands.

Archival newsreel footage of the Normandy Invasion can be seen at this website.

PS

archive video D-Day

A Personal Perspective

Claus Fuhrmann lived in Berlin when Russian troops entered the city. Berliners had been hiding in cellars for weeks. Fuhrmann described what happened when Russian soldiers made food supplies available on May 1, 1945. "The cellars . . . became the scene of an incredible spectacle. The starving people flung themselves like beasts over one another, shouting, pushing and struggling to lay their hands on whatever they could. . . . In order not to be trampled down themselves the Russians fired . . . into the crowds with machine-pistols, killing several."[2]

THE LIBERATION OF EUROPE

D-Day marked the beginning of the liberation of Europe, but it would take another 11 months before Germany finally surrendered. Before the end came, one momentous event followed another.

The Allies liberated Paris on August 25, 1944. The next day, General Charles de Gaulle paraded with troops down the Champs-Élysées. Fighting continued in the Pacific, with General Douglas MacArthur returning to the Philippines on October 20, 1944.

In December 1944, Germany staged a surprise offensive in the forests of France and Belgium. Called the Battle of the Bulge, because the Axis forces created a "bulge" in the Allied frontlines, it claimed the lives of thousands. The battle may have delayed the advance of Allied troops into Germany, but the high German losses of men and equipment made it easier for the western Allies in the end.

While the Allies had been bombing military targets in German cities since 1942, in February 1945, the Allies began bombing cities that were full of civilians, in the hopes of demoralizing the German people and creating confusion. Dresden is one example of a German city that suffered significant civilian deaths in the last year of war. Here, an estimated 25,000 people died in a firestorm.

On April 12, 1945, President Roosevelt died of a brain hemorrhage, just months after being elected to a fourth term. Vice President Harry S. Truman (1884–1972) took Roosevelt's place.

On April 28, 1945, Italian partisans shot and killed Benito Mussolini. When they hung his body in a public square in Milan, crowds gathered. They vented their rage against their former dictator by attacking the corpse until Mussolini's face was unrecognizable.

That same month, Russian troops captured Berlin. They hoped to take Adolf Hitler, but he committed suicide by shooting himself in his bunker under the chancellery building. In a garden outside the chancellery, Hitler's supporters poured gasoline over his corpse and burned it to ashes. Why was it important to his supporters to destroy the body?

LIBERATION OF THE CAMPS

Of all the events that were watched by the world at the end of the war, nothing compared to the awful sights of the Nazi concentration camps and killing centers. Rumors of German atrocities had circulated throughout the war, but few Allied soldiers were prepared for the inhumanity that they witnessed in places such as Auschwitz or Dachau.

They came upon thousands of corpses rotting in piles on the ground. They found prisoners so emaciated they could count every bone in their bodies. Others were too weak to lift themselves from filthy wooden bunk beds.

Children who survived Auschwitz

credit: United States Holocaust Memorial Museum, courtesy of Belarusian State Archive of Documentary Film and Photography

HELPERS

To save Jewish lives, some people risked punishment, even death, at the hands of the Nazis. You can read testimonies from these people at these websites. Why would they take the risk? What makes them different from people who did nothing to help?

PS

Rescue and Resistance USHMM

Yad Vashem stories

Some Allied soldiers were so upset they executed SS guards on the spot. Some prisoners, if they had the strength, also took their revenge. The main job, though, was helping those who still lived and burying those who had died. Neither job was easy.

Soldiers often tried to share food with the starving men and women they'd found, but often this backfired. Starving people usually lack the physical ability to digest normal foods. The emaciated victims would eat chocolate bars, canned goods, and bread, only to get violently sick right afterward. For some, the shock of food on their weakened systems resulted in death.

It was also incredibly difficult to properly bury the dead. Allied troops were overwhelmed by the sheer numbers of corpses. Even soldiers who were hardened by years of combat struggled to cope in the face of so much slaughter.

The Holocaust Revealed

As evidence of the Holocaust reached the public, many people reacted with disbelief. Verbal reports given on the radio were at first rejected as being too outrageous to be believed. Photographs from Nazi camps were deemed too ghastly to be printed. Soon, however, exhibitions of Nazi camp photographs were put on display for people to view. Many people came away from the exhibits forever changed by what they saw.

VICTORY IN THE PACIFIC

Peace came to Europe when Germany surrendered on May 8, 1945. In the Pacific Ocean, however, fighting continued without pause.

> The question on everyone's mind was, "Will the Japanese ever surrender?" Many feared they would not.

The cost of war to the Japanese people had been tremendous and many longed for peace. But at the highest level of Japanese leadership, surrender was out of the question.

BATTLE WATCH

The Japanese surrendered on August 15, 1945, but Japan did not sign official terms of surrender until September 2, aboard the USS *Missouri*.

Japan held out even after President Truman authorized the first-ever use of an atomic bomb over the city of Hiroshima on August 6, 1945. The attack flattened the city and added tens of thousands more civilian deaths to Japan's growing list of casualties.

Japanese leadership declined to surrender even three days later, when President Truman ordered a second atomic bomb to be released on the city of Nagasaki. That same day, Russia declared war on Japan. They sent troops into the northern Chinese area of Manchuria, which the Japanese had ruled as Manchukuo since 1932.

Japan's military leaders still refused to give up. How much more could the people of Japan take?

Another week passed before Emperor Hirohito acted. Having allowed the military to lead the Japanese people to the brink of annihilation, Hirohito finally took control of the situation. On August 15, 1945, in a recorded radio address, Hirohito announced the Japanese surrendered.

The Pacific War was over.

KEY QUESTIONS

- **What challenges did Allied leaders face as they prepared to bring World War II to an end?**
- **Why did fighting continue in Italy even after the Italian government signed an armistice?**
- **What effect do you think secrecy played in President Truman's use of nuclear weapons?**

Using the Atomic Bomb

President Truman's use of nuclear weapons has always generated controversy. There was little public debate at the time, however.

From a military standpoint, some historians argue that nuclear weapons brought the fighting to an early end and reduced further American casualties. Others claim that Japan was already so weakened by the war that conventional weapons would have brought hostilities to an end just as quickly.

People also question whether the use of nuclear weapons was morally justifiable. Conventional bombs killed millions of people during the war, but the radiation fallout from nuclear weapons continued to harm people for decades after the war ended.

Inquire & Investigate

THE NUCLEAR DEBATE

Do you think President Truman's decision to use nuclear weapons was justifiable, either militarily or morally?

- **Stage a debate among your classmates or friends in which you argue for or against Truman's decision.** Conduct your research online and at the library. Come up with three to five points in support of your position.
- **Consider these questions in your research.**
  - Is there evidence that Japan was ready to surrender before the bombs were dropped?
  - Did Japan's conduct during the war justify extreme measures?
  - Is there evidence that nuclear weapons were no more destructive than fire bombing?
  - Is there a "right" or "wrong" way to kill civilians during a war?
  - How did the scientists who developed the atomic bomb feel about what they created?
- **Did your original opinion change after you listened to both sides of the debate?** Why or why not?

To investigate more, read newspapers and news magazines for stories about nuclear weapons today. Which countries have them? Are efforts being made to reduce their numbers? Is there a danger that nuclear weapons might be used again?

VOCAB LAB

Write down what you think each word means. What root words can you find to help you? What does the context of the word tell you?

atrocity, **atomic bomb**, **casualties**, **convoy**, **emaciated**, **inhumanity**, **liberation**, **partisan**, and **strategic**.

Compare your definitions with those of your friends or classmates. Did you all come up with the same meanings? Turn to the text and glossary if you need help.

Chapter 7
Legacies of World War II

What lasting effect has World War II had on the world?

Many countries banded together to prevent the atrocities of World War II and the Holocaust from ever happening again, but a complete and lasting peace is still out of reach.

By mid-August 1945, hostilities in both Europe and the Pacific had officially ended. The war was won and everyone looked forward to resuming normal lives. But could the world ever be normal again?

Millions of people were homeless. Cities and economies were in ruins. National boundaries had been redrawn and colonial empires were crumbling. Old institutions that had failed to maintain peace were replaced by new institutions with no proven track record. It would take years, billions of dollars, and an international commitment to diplomacy before the world would discover its new normal.

THE WANDERING MILLIONS

When the fighting stopped, millions of people suddenly flooded Europe's highways, all searching for a path home. Who were these wandering millions? And where were they going?

Some of them were slave laborers that Germany had forcefully relocated from all corners of Europe. Others were Allied and Axis POWs. There were also exiled Germans who were no longer welcome in the formerly German parts of Poland. Plus, 200,000 Jewish survivors of the Nazi death camps and Jews who had gone into hiding or had fled to the relative safety of Russia joined the massive crowds. Everyone was searching for a place to call home.

But where was home? That was an enormous challenge. The sheer logistics of transporting people was part of the problem, since many bridges, roads, and railroads had been damaged during the war. There were political and social problems as well.

Some people did not want to go home. For example, Russia's leaders treated soldiers who had surrendered as traitors. When word spread that Russian POWs were being shot or imprisoned as soon as they reached Russian soil, many decided they'd rather stay where they were.

Polish refugees often feared going home, too. In the political turmoil of the time, Poland came under the influence of communist Russia. Many Poles feared life under the rule of Joseph Stalin. His cruelty and ruthlessness were well known.

The United Nations Relief and Rehabilitation Administration (UNRRA) was tasked with sorting out these complex issues. At its peak, the UNRRA employed 12,000 people. They helped 7 million victims of war with housing, food, medical treatment, job training, and transportation. By 1947, the UNRRA operated 800 resettlement camps across Europe and Asia.

Displaced Persons in Asia

Europe was not the only place flooded with displaced persons at the end of World War II. In Asia and the Pacific islands, the numbers were equally overwhelming. Like Germany, Japan had filled its labor needs through enslavement. They exploited more than 1 million Koreans and millions more POWs. Scattered throughout Japan, China, Indonesia, and Burma, these people had to find a way home.

More than 6 million Japanese soldiers and civilians were also dispersed throughout the region. Like their counterparts in Europe, they wandered through the countryside and ruined cities, and they often found their homes destroyed. Many people blamed Japanese soldiers for the terrible war and met returning men with anger and violence.

A child survivor of the Buchenwald concentration camp

credit: USHMM

A Personal Perspective

Alan Moorehead (1910-1983) was a World War II correspondent. He reported on the appearance of liberated slave laborers in Germany. "Little groups of Frenchmen, then Dutch, then Belgians and Czechs and Poles and Italians, and finally, in overwhelming majority, the Russians in their bright green uniforms. . . . Half the nationalities of Europe were on the march, all moving blindly westward along the roads. . . . They wore the striped prison garb of the concentration camps . . . or the scummiest rags. All along the highways lay little bundles of incredibly filthy and smelly tatters discarded by the slaves who found something better."[1]

NO PLACE TO CALL HOME

Unique among Europe's displaced persons were the 1.5 million Jews scattered across the continent. In theory, they had homes to return to. In reality, much of their property had been claimed by non-Jewish citizens, who refused to give it back.

Those Jews whose homes were waiting for them often encountered hostility on their return. The war had ended, but racism and anti-Semitism still formed the attitudes of some people. Communities that had applauded the removal of their Jewish neighbors did not welcome them back with open arms.

To make matters worse, countries that could have provided refuge to Europe's Jews failed to do so. The United States, Great Britain, Canada, and others severely limited the number of Jews allowed into their countries. Where could these people go where they'd be accepted and allowed to start a new life?

THE BIRTH OF ISRAEL

The region of Palestine had long played a central role in the history of the Jews. In Biblical times, Jews built their Holy Temple in the city of Jerusalem, making it the heart of their religious community. War and persecution had dispersed the Jews throughout the world, but Palestine had always been thought of as a true home. This was especially true after the Holocaust.

But Palestine was not a perfect solution. Native Arab Palestinians pushed back against the crowds of Jewish immigrants who were moving there. Armed conflicts erupted.

In 1945, the United Nations (UN) had come into existence to maintain world peace. Two years later, the new organization hoped to settle the Jewish-Palestinian conflict by dividing Palestine between the Jews and the Arab Palestinians.

Arab Palestinians objected to the unequal division of their ancestral lands, but the UN did little to address their concerns. On May 14, 1948, Israel declared itself an independent country.

The Jews finally had a home, but they did not have peace. The day after Israel declared statehood, a group of Arab nations attacked the new country. The Arab-Israeli war lasted 10 months. When it was over, Israel controlled nearly 80 percent of all Palestinian lands.

Between the creation of Israel and the war, more than 750,000 Arab Palestinians were forced from their homes into refugee camps. Meanwhile, the same number of Jews had to leave Arab countries, and many of them settled in Israel. The conflict between Israelis and Palestinians has continued ever since and remains unresolved today.

BATTLE WATCH

In defeat, Japan was required to give up control of Korea. The United States administered South Korea and Russia administered North Korea. By 1950, North and South Korea were at war.

Listen to David Ben-Gurion, Israel's founding father, announce the birth of Israel. He speaks in Hebrew, but English subtitles are provided.

PS

Israel Declaration Independence

ECONOMIC REVIVAL

With much of Europe and Asia in ruins, the country best able to lend assistance was the United States. Political leaders came up with the Marshall Plan, which provided 18 European countries, including Germany, with billions of dollars. With this infusion of money, poverty and starvation were greatly reduced, and industrial and agricultural production increased dramatically.

In Japan, the United States staved off starvation by providing millions of dollars in food aid and setting up a new food distribution network. With General Douglas MacArthur at the helm, Japan remained under U.S. control until 1952. As in Europe, the Japanese economy recovered quickly. In particular, Japan saw tremendous growth in the manufacture and sale of automobiles and electronic goods. How many brands of Japanese cars can you think of?

OCCUPIED GERMANY

From 1945 to 1949, the Allied powers divided Germany into four administrative zones: American, French, British, and Russian. Citizens in each zone lived under the governmental policies of the occupying Allied force. The long-term goal, however, was for Germany to become a unified country. Those plans went astray, however, when political disagreements arose between communist Russia and the Western democracies. In 1949, the western zones combined to form the democratic Republic of Germany (West Germany), while the eastern Russian zone became the communist German Democratic Republic (East Germany).

There was little democracy in East Germany. Its people lived under the rules of communist Russia, where freedoms were limited.

SEEKING JUSTICE

After the war, people wanted justice. Terrible crimes had been committed, and bringing the worst offenders to account for their actions was a top priority of the Allied powers.

Where to lay the blame, however, was a complicated affair.

Not every Nazi Party member in Germany was a criminal, and not all of those who were criminals—such as members of the Einsatzgruppen—could be brought to trial. Complete justice was an impossible goal. Compromises had to be made.

Beginning in 1945, partial justice was achieved in a series of war tribunals held in Nuremberg, Germany, known as the Nuremberg Trials. In these proceedings, major Nazi figures were charged with "crimes against humanity." This was a new legal term, used to describe the wide scope and harsh brutality of the Nazi regime.

Not everyone who stood accused in Nuremberg was found guilty. Of the first 22 Nazi leaders brought to trial, three were acquitted. The 19 men who were convicted faced the death penalty, life imprisonment, or prison sentences of 10 to 20 years.

In Japan, the biggest debate was about Emperor Hirohito. Was he responsible for Japan's involvement in World War II? An entire nation had pledged devotion to their emperor. During the war, soldiers believed that orders from their superior officers came from the emperor himself.

Soldiers had been ordered to massacre and rape innocent civilians and to torture POWs. Who was responsible, the soldiers, the emperor, or the military leaders whose advice Hirohito had followed?

Some argued that Emperor Hirohito should be charged with war crimes, but that never happened. Hirohito remained the emperor of Japan until his death in 1989.

At the International Military Tribunal for the Far East, held in Tokyo in 1946, people other than Emperor Hirohito shouldered the blame for Japan's wrongdoings. Australia, China, the Netherlands, France, the United States, the Philippines, and Great Britain all held trials. Thousands of people were held accountable for crimes ranging from murder to inhumane medical experiments.

THE BERLIN WALL

From 1961 to 1989, the Berlin Wall separated East and West Germany. The main purpose of the Berlin Wall was to prevent East Germans from leaving their communist country in search of freedom in West Germany. Armed guards patrolled the Berlin Wall with orders to shoot anyone attempting to leave. In 1989, however, political unrest resulted in the demise of the Berlin Wall. On November 9, 1989, the East German government announced that people could move freely between the two countries. Almost immediately, crowds of East Germans went through the Berlin Wall and took advantage of their new freedom. By October 1990, Germany once again was a unified country. The Berlin Wall has since been demolished.

INTERNATIONAL COOPERATION

Watch a live news report of East and West Berliners as they begin to tear down the Berlin Wall.

PS

Berlin Wall falls video

Even before the Second World War ended, Allied leaders sought to create a new international order based on diplomacy rather than war. Similar efforts had been made at the end of World War I, too. But the League of Nations, formed in 1920 with the mission to ensure world peace, had failed. What would work?

The UN was created to take its place.

The UN got its start in 1941, when President Roosevelt and Prime Minister Churchill coauthored a document known as the Atlantic Charter.

The Atlantic Charter outlined the major goals that the Allies hoped to achieve at the end of the war. These included the self-determination of nations, the right of people to be free of fear and want, global economic cooperation, the disarmament of hostile nations, and an end to the use of force.

BATTLE WATCH

Many leading Nazis escaped punishment by taking their own lives. They included Adolf Hitler, Hermann Göring, Joseph Goebbels, Heinrich Himmler, and Martin Bormann.

The UN headquarters in New York City

credit: Dendodge

Those policies formed the foundation of the UN, which officially began operations in October 1945 at its headquarters in New York City. Today, the UN's core mission remains the same—to maintain world peace. But the UN also promotes human rights, protects the environment, and gives aid in times of famine, natural disaster, and war.

THE EUROPEAN UNION

Having endured two devastating wars in just 31 years, many Europeans sought an end to a Europe where nations endlessly competed against one another. They worked toward a unified Europe, a federation of states ruled by mutual assistance.

Forging a new Europe was a slow process. It started in the 1950s with some economic cooperation among six nations—Italy, France, Belgium, Luxembourg, West Germany, and the Netherlands. As time went on, more than 20 other countries joined what became the European Union (EU) in 1993.

Today, these countries cooperate in many different ways. Most EU countries share a common currency, the euro. Borders are open so people can travel freely from one country to another and work in a member EU country.

Today, the EU includes 28 countries, but many people worry about its durability. Old conflicts have emerged anew. While Germany has demonstrated an openness to refugees, it is again the economic powerhouse of the continent. Smaller countries with weak economies, such as Greece, sometimes feel threatened by the oversized influence that Germany wields. In turn, Germany sometimes resents its obligations to less successful neighbors.

DEMOCRACY IN JAPAN

After the war, imperial Japan was replaced with a parliamentary style democracy. Japan created a new constitution, which took absolute power away from the emperor and gave it to the people.

Japan's first post-war elections took place on April 10, 1946. For the first time in Japanese history, women were allowed to vote. Along with their male countrymen, they chose Shigeru Yoshida (1878–1967) to be their first democratically elected prime minister.

The biggest challenge to the survival of a unified Europe came in 2016, when Great Britain voted to leave the EU. Britain has been a member of the European Union since 1973. How its departure will affect the EU is one of the great political questions of our time.

External and internal disruptions also tear at the delicate fabric of the European Union. European countries are challenged with finding humane and fiscally responsible ways of helping a steady flow of refugees coming to them from war-torn countries in the Middle East and Africa. They are also confronted with homegrown white supremacist movements. Demanding an end to immigration, dreaming of a more Aryan Europe, these new nationalist groups are direct descendants of the Nazi Party.

BATTLE WATCH

In the decades following World War II, dozens of countries gained independence from colonial rule. India was first, winning its independence from Great Britain in 1947.

KEY QUESTIONS

- **How might the special circumstances of Europe's Jews have been handled differently?**
- **Should Emperor Hirohito have been held responsible for Japan's criminal actions during the war?**
- **What are some of the challenges of a unified Europe?**

AFTER THE STORM

The two great world wars of the twentieth century passed like violent storms across the face of the globe. The world survived, and awoke to a new day with most nations more committed than ever to peaceful coexistence. But from the wreckage of those awful wars, pressing new questions have emerged.

Will the relative peace in Europe hold? Will the Israelis and the Palestinians ever bridge their differences? Will nuclear weapons be used again? Will new dictators gain the power to shake the foundations of the earth?

Those questions—and more—are the legacy of World War II.

THE WORLD AT WAR

The UN has endured, but it has not achieved world peace. Around the world, wars continue to be fought. Where are armed conflicts taking place today? What are the attackers and defenders fighting about?

- **Search through several newspapers or magazines to find articles or editorials about armed conflicts around the world.**
    - How many articles did you find?
    - Which nations are at war?
    - Can you describe what these countries are fighting about?
- **Some people believe that the UN is no longer relevant and should be dismantled.** What do you think? Discuss the issue among your classmates or friends, or design a presentation that explains your point of view.

To investigate more, spend some time exploring the UN website. In addition to promoting peace, what else does the UN try to accomplish in the world?

United Nations

VOCAB LAB

Write down what you think each word means. What root words can you find to help you? What does the context of the word tell you?

acquit, **coexistence**, **disarmament**, **displaced person**, **justice**, **human rights**, **refugee**, **self-determination**, **slave laborer**, **traitor**, and **war tribunal**.

Compare your definitions with those of your friends or classmates. Did you all come up with the same meanings? Turn to the text and glossary if you need help.

REFUGEES AND DISPLACED PERSONS

War, famine, and natural disasters still drive people from their homes. Who are today's refugees and displaced persons?

- **Search through several newspapers or magazines to find articles or editorials about refugees or displaced persons.**
  - Where are refugee crises taking place today?
  - What is causing people to flee their homes?
  - Can refugees find countries willing to take them in?
  - See how many refugees were settled in the United States and where they found new homes in 2016.

states with most refugees

- **Choose one of the refugee groups you read about in the news.** Write up a report or create a presentation about the group.

To investigate more, visit the website of the UN High Commission for Refugees and read some of the stories about today's refugees.

UNHCR

Inquire & Investigate

WHY DO WE BUILD WALLS?

The Berlin Wall is just one example of the dividing structures that human beings have been building for thousands of years. Ancient structures include Hadrian's Wall in northern Britain and the Great Wall in China. Newer structures include the West Bank Wall in Israel and a wall that separates the border between Bulgaria and Turkey.

- **Undertake a small research project on one old and one new wall.**
  - Which country built the wall?
  - For what purpose was the wall constructed?
  - Did it succeed in what it was set up to do?
- **Create a presentation based on your findings and share them with your classmates or friends.** Do people today build walls for the same reasons that they did in the past? Has their construction over the centuries changed or stayed the same?
- **Read Robert Frost's famous poem about maintaining a wall between himself and his neighbor.** The poem is called "Mending Wall." What does the poem say about the purpose of walls? Does Robert Frost approve of them or is he uncertain about them?

Mending Wall

To investigate more, explore President Donald Trump's 2017 proposal to build a wall between Mexico and the United States. What is the status of that proposal today? What are the pros and cons of building such a structure? Are you for or against the construction of a wall between the United States and Mexico?

GLOSSARY

abdicate: to step down as the ruler of a country, or give up a position of authority.

acquit: to find someone not guilty of a criminal charge.

advocate: to publicly support.

agenda: a list of things to be done or goals to be reached.

aggression: hostile or violent behavior against another person or a group of people.

alliance: an agreement between or among countries to work together toward a common goal.

Allied powers: the countries that fought together against Germany and the Axis powers during World War II, including Great Britain, the Soviet Union, and the United States.

ally: a partner in an alliance.

ancestral: belonging to or inherited from one's ancestors.

annex: to take possession of a land or a country, usually by force.

annihilation: complete destruction.

anti-Semitism: prejudice or hostility toward Jewish people.

armistice: an official agreement between enemies to stop fighting.

arson: the deliberate and illegal setting of a fire.

artillery: large firearms used in war.

Aryan: a non-Jewish person of northern European or Germanic descent.

atomic bomb: a bomb that is powered by the nuclear energy released by splitting an atom.

atrocity: a cruel act of violence.

Axis powers: the countries of Germany, Italy, and Japan, which fought against the Allies during World War II.

barren: not capable of producing life.

bayonet: a sword-like blade fixed to the end of a gun for hand-to-hand fighting.

Blitz: the German air raids on Britain in 1940–1941.

blitzkrieg: a German term for "lightning war," indicating a quick and decisive military victory.

blockade: closing off a place or port to prevent entry or exit.

Bolshevism: the communist form of government adopted by Russia after the revolution of 1917.

boycott: refusing to buy or sell goods as part of a protest.

brainwash: to use psychological and/or physical pressure to force someone to accept beliefs that they would not normally accept.

brazen: bold and without shame.

capitalism: an economic and political system where products and services are controlled by individuals rather than by the government.

capitulate: surrender.

casualties: people killed or injured in battle.

census: an official count of a population.

Central powers: a group of countries that fought against the Allies in WWI, including Germany, Austria-Hungary, Bulgaria, and the Ottoman Empire.

chaos: a state of complete confusion.

charter: a document that spells out the goals and rights of an organization or city.

citizen: a person who legally belongs to a country and has the rights and protection of that country.

civilian: a person who is not in the military.

civilization: a community of people that is advanced in art, science, and government.

coexistence: living together.

colonize: to take control of an area and the people who live there.

colony: a country or area that is under the political control of another country.

commendation: an award for exemplary behavior or service.

commission: a group of people officially charged with performing a set list of tasks.

communism: a system of government in which everything is owned and run by the government.

concentration camp: during WWII, large camps where Jews and other minorities were imprisoned by the Nazis and forced to perform hard labor or exterminated.

conscientious objector: a person who refuses to fight in a war due to personal or religious beliefs.

conscription: the drafting of men into military service.

constitution: a document containing the basic laws and beliefs of a country.

controversy: a public disagreement between two sides.

conventional: ordinary.

converge: to come together.

convoy: a group of ships or vehicles traveling together, typically protected by armed troops, warships, or other vehicles.

corpse: a dead body.

cremate: to burn the body of a person who has died.

crematorium: a place where corpses are burned to ashes in large ovens.

culture: the beliefs and way of life of a group of people.

debt: something that is owed.

decadent: a state of moral or cultural decline, or something that is richly extravagant.

dehydration: the dangerous loss of body fluids.

demise: end.

democracy: a system of government elected freely by the people where citizens have a say in how things are run.

demoralize: to cause someone to lose hope or to feel helpless.

deprivation: not having the things needed for a comfortable or healthy life.

descendant: related to someone who lived in the past.

destabilization: causing unrest or keeping something such as a government from operating in the normal way.

dictator: a ruler with total control over a country, particularly one who has gotten that power through force.

dictatorship: a form of government where one leader controls all aspects of a country.

diplomacy: the nonviolent management of international relations.

disarmament: getting rid of one's weapons.

disperse: to scatter over a wide area.

displaced person: a person who has lost their home due to acts of nature or war.

divine: related to God or a god.

documentary: a story about true events.

domino effect: an event in one country that causes similar events in neighboring countries, like a falling domino causing other upright dominoes to fall.

drafted: required to join the military.

draftee: a person called up for military service.

drone: an unmanned aerial vehicle.

Eastern Front: during World War I, the fighting that took place in the east between the Russian Empire on one side and the Central powers on the other.

economy: the wealth and resources of an area or country.

Einsatzgruppen: the German mobile killing squads used by the Nazi army during World War II.

elaborate: complicated in design or planning.

elite: those viewed as the most important people.

emaciated: abnormally thin or weak.

embroil: to involve someone deeply in a difficult situation.

empire: a group of countries, states, or lands that are ruled by one ruler.

enlist: to sign up for military service.

epidemic: an illness that affects large numbers of people.

eradicate: to entirely wipe out.

European Union: the European countries legally banded together for mutual support.

execution: put to death.

GLOSSARY

exile: being banned from your country, especially for political reasons or as a punishment.

exploit: to make full use of something in a way that almost has a negative connotation.

extermination camp: a camp where entire groups of people are killed.

evacuation: leaving an area due to an emergency such as fire, flooding, or war.

fallout: radioactive particles released into the air after a nuclear explosion.

famine: a period of great hunger and lack of food for a large population.

fanaticism: excessive enthusiasm or obsession.

fascism: a form of government that considers the nation more important than the individual and maintains total control over its citizens' lives.

fascist: a follower of fascism.

federation: a group of states with central government but local independence.

feudal: a society in which a few people own the land and have power over others.

fire bombing: bombing that sets things on fire and does not aim to hit a specified target.

formidable: large, powerful, and difficult to defeat.

fuel efficient: operating on small amounts of fuel.

führer: a leader with the unlimited powers of a dictator.

futility: pointlessness.

genocide: the deliberate killing of a large group of people based on race, ethnicity, or nationality.

geography: the features of a place, such as mountains and rivers.

Germanic: relating to Germany and its people.

global: relating to the entire world.

Great Depression: a worldwide economic crisis that lasted from October 1929 to 1939.

harmony: peace and agreement.

heir: a person entitled to receive property upon the death of another.

Holocaust: a time before and during World War II when the German Nazis tried to kill the entire Jewish race, as well as several other groups.

homosexual: a person who is sexually attracted to others of the same gender.

hostility: anger or violence directed at another.

human rights: basic rights that belong to every person.

hypnotic: having a trancelike effect or quality.

immerse: to involve deeply in an activity or idea.

immigrant: a person who comes to settle in a new country.

impediment: something that gets in the way.

imperial: of or relating to an empire.

impromptu: done without planning.

incendiary: a device designed to cause fires.

industrialize: to change from manufacturing goods by hand to producing products in factories.

inevitable: certain to happen.

infamy: well known for doing or being something bad.

infantry: soldiers who fight on foot.

infection: illness caused by a bacteria or virus.

inferior: lower in rank, status, or quality.

inflation: a rise in the cost of goods at the same time as the purchasing value of money goes down.

infrastructure: roads, bridges, and other basic types of structures and equipment needed for a country to function properly.

infuriate: to make extremely angry.

infusion: the sudden and usually large introduction of a new element into a situation.

inglorious: causing shame or a loss of honor.

inhumanity: cruelty or brutal behavior.

innovation: a new device, idea, or method.

instigate: to set an action or event into motion.

insulate: to shield or protect from outside influences.

intelligence: information that is gathered or known about an enemy or potential enemy.

internment camp: a prison or detention camp used during wartime.

interracial: involving one or more human races.

irrational: not logical or reasonable.

island hopping: in World War II, advancing from one island to the next until a destination is reached.

isolationism: the policy of remaining apart from other countries and not getting involved in their affairs.

Jew: a person who is Jewish, who practices Judaism.

Judaism: a religion developed by ancient Hebrews who believed in one god. Followers of Judaism are called Jews.

justice: fair action or treatment based on the law.

kaiser: the German emperor.

kamikaze: Japanese pilots who performed suicide missions by crashing their aircraft, loaded with explosives, into enemy targets.

Kristallnacht: in German, the "Night of Broken Glass," the name given to anti-Semitic rioting in Germany on November 9–10, 1938.

lebensraum: a German word that refers to the idea that the nation's survival depends on it being able to expand through colonization.

legacy: the lasting influence of a person or event.

liberation: being set free, especially from slavery or imprisonment.

loot: property taken from an enemy in war.

Luftwaffe: the German air force.

machinist: a skilled worker who operates machines, especially in the making of tools.

malnourished: not receiving adequate amounts of food or nutrients.

mandatory: required.

manipulation: controlling and influencing someone cleverly or unfairly.

Marxism: a political philosophy based on the idea that workers should overthrow capitalist forms of government.

merciless: showing no pity or humanity.

mesmerize: to hold a person or people as if in a trance.

minority: a smaller subset of a larger group of people.

mobilize: to prepare a military.

monarchy: a government ruled by a monarch, such as a king or queen.

morality: having to do with right and wrong behavior.

mortar: a short, smoothbore gun used for firing shells (bombs) at high angles.

munitions: military weapons, ammunition, or equipment.

nationalism: an extreme form of patriotism.

natural resource: something found in nature that is useful to humans, such as water to drink, trees to burn, and fish to eat.

naval: related to the navy.

Nazi: a member of the National Socialist German Workers' Party, the ruling political party of Germany before and during World War II.

neutral: not taking sides in a conflict.

Nisei: second-generation Japanese Americans, some of whom served in the U.S. armed forces in World War II.

No Man's Land: in World War I, the physical area located between two sides of a war zone.

noncombatant: a person who is not engaged in fighting during a war, especially a civilian, chaplain, or medical practitioner.

Nordic: relating to the countries of Germany and Scandinavia.

GLOSSARY

nuclear bomb: a powerful bomb fueled by the energy released from the splitting of atoms.

nurture: to care for and encourage the growth of a person or idea.

obscure: not discovered or known about.

occupation: in war, the act of invading and then controlling another country.

orator: a public speaker.

pacifist: someone who does not believe in violence or war.

pact: a formal agreement.

panzer: a German word for any type of armored tank used in World War II.

paramilitary: an unofficial fighting force that operates outside of government control.

parliament: in some governments, the group of people responsible for making laws.

partisan: a member of an armed group that fights secretly against an occupying force.

patriotism: devotion to and love for one's country.

peninsula: a piece of land that juts out into water.

persecution: to treat people cruelly or unfairly because of their membership in a social, racial, religious, ethnic, or political group.

perspective: a person's point of view.

pillbox: in war, a small, enclosed structure from which soldiers fire their weapons.

plight: a dangerous, difficult, or unfortunate situation.

precision bombing: bombing with the aim of hitting a specified target.

prejudice: an opinion about another person that is not based on reason or experience.

prolong: to keep something going.

propaganda: ideas or statements that are sometimes exaggerated or even false. They are spread to help a cause, political leader, or government.

racial cleansing: removing or killing a particular race of people from a country.

racism: an irrational hatred of people based on race.

radiation: electromagnetic particles that impair human health.

rationale: the reasons given for why an action is undertaken.

rationing: in a time of shortage, limiting the amount of food and other goods (such as gasoline) that people can buy.

rearmament: acquiring or building up a new supply of weapons.

recruit: a person enlisted into military service.

refuge: safety.

refugee: a person forced to leave his or her native land to seek safety, usually as a result of war or persecution.

Reichstag: the German parliament, both the officials and the building they used.

reinforce: to make stronger.

reparations: compensation from one country to another for war damages.

resilient: able to recover from physical or mental injury.

resistance: a fight to prevent something from happening.

retaliation: fighting back in response to an attack.

revolution: a sudden and important change.

revolutionary: markedly new or introducing radical change, or a person fighting for radical change.

ritual suicide: taking your own life for reasons other than personal despair.

robust: healthy, strong, vibrant.

Romani: a member of a group of people in Europe living a nomadic life, moving from place to place. Often referred to as gypsies.

ruthless: showing no mercy, having no pity or compassion.

sacrifice: to give up something valuable for the good of another.

sanctions: threatened penalties for disobeying a law or rule, usually imposed on a country by another country.

segregate: to separate people based on race, religion, ethnicity, or some other category.

self-determination: deciding for yourself what you want to do, or a country deciding its fate free of outside interference.

self-sufficient: not needing help from others.

shell: in military terms, a bomb filled with explosive charge that is fired from a gun, often a mortar, but generally a piece of artillery.

siege: surrounding a place, such as a city, to cut off supplies and help force surrender.

simultaneous: happening or being done at the same time.

slave laborer: a person who is performing unpaid labor under threat.

sniper: a person who shoots from a hiding place.

socialism: a political, social, and economic system meant to empower the working class.

stalemate: a contest where neither side is winning.

strategic: carefully planned in order to achieve a particular aim.

strike: an organized protest in which people refuse to work until changes are made in the workplace. Also a military action.

strongman: a person who gets things done through intimidation or violence.

stymie: to prevent or hinder progress.

subhuman: less than human or not worthy of a human being.

subterranean: below the surface of the earth.

superior: higher in rank or better in quality.

swastika: the symbol of the Nazis and Nazi Germany.

technology: the tools, methods, and systems used to solve a problem or do work.

terminology: language, terms, or phrases, especially as used in a particular business or field of study.

terrain: land or ground and all of its physical features, such as hills, rocks, and water.

territory: an area of land.

testimony: the statement of a witness.

Third Reich: the third German empire, which consisted of Nazi control from 1933 to 1945.

thwart: to stop something from being accomplished.

traitor: someone who betrays their country.

treaty: a formal agreement between countries.

tribunal: a court of justice.

troops: large groups of soldiers.

turmoil: great confusion or uncertainty.

unanimous: when a decision or action is agreed upon by everyone involved.

United Nations: a global organization in which countries work together for the common good.

vandalize: to deliberately destroy or damage property.

venue: the place where a planned event happens.

victory garden: gardens planted and maintained in both public and private spaces during times of war.

warmonger: a person who wants their country to go to war without good cause to do so.

war tribunal: a court where charges are brought against people accused of committing crimes during times of war.

Wehrmacht: the German armed forces.

Western Front: In World War II, the fighting that took place in Belgium and France between the Allied powers and Germany.

white supremacy: a person who holds the racist belief that white people are superior to those of all other races.

Zimmerman Telegram: in 1917, a telegram in which Germany sought an alliance with Mexico, and urged Mexico to reclaim territory from the United States.

RESOURCES

BOOKS

Beevor, Antony. *The Second World War.* Little, Brown and Company, 2012.

Bennis, Phyllis. *Understanding the Palestinian-Israeli Conflict: A Primer.* Olive Branch Press, 2007.

Buruma, Ian. *Year Zero: A History of 1945.* Penguin Books, 2013.

Carey, John, ed. *Eyewitness to History.* Harvard University Press, 1987.

Murray, Williamson and Millett, Allan R. *A War to Be Won: Fighting the Second World War.* Belknap Press, 2000.

Shephard, Ben. *The Long Road Home: The Aftermath of the Second World War.* Alfred A. Knopf, 2011.

Tuchman, Barbara W. *The Guns of August: The Outbreak of World War I.* Tess Press, 2005.

Ward, Geoffrey C. and Burns, Ken. *The War: An Intimate History 1941-1945.* Alfred A. Knopf, 2007.

Webster, Donovan. *The Burma Road: The Epic Story of the China-Burma-India Theater in World War II.* Farrar, Strauss and Giroux, 2003.

Weinberg, Gerhard L. *A World at Arms: A Global History of World War II.* Cambridge University Press, 1994.

MUSEUMS

The National World War II Museum, in New Orleans, Louisiana
nationalww2museum.org

The International Museum of World War II, in Natick, Massachusetts
museumofworldwarii.org

Heart Mountain: World War II Japanese American Confinement Site, in Powell, Wyoming
heartmountain.org

United States Holocaust Memorial Museum, in Washington, D.C.
ushmm.org

War in the Pacific National Historical Park, in Asan, Guam
pacifichistoricparks.org

WEBSITES

PBS website based on the Ken Burns film, *The War: An Intimate History 1941-1945*
pbs.org/thewar

Encyclopedia of the Second World War
spartacus-educational.com/2WW.htm

BBC Online: World War II
bbc.co.uk/history/worldwars/wwtwo

VIDEOS

Tiffin, Peter. *World at War.*

BBC Video. *D-Day: Reflections of Courage.*

SOURCE NOTES

INTRODUCTION

1 Carey, John, ed. *Eyewitness to History*. Harvard University Press, 1987.

CHAPTER 1

1 Bernhardi, General Friedrich von. *Germany and the Next War.* E. Arnold, 1914.

2 Carey, John, ed. *Eyewitness to History*. Harvard University Press, 1987.

CHAPTER 2

1 N.H. Baynes, ed. *The Speeches of Adolf Hitler, Vol. I*, Howard Fertig, 1942.

2 Carey, John, ed. *Eyewitness to History*. Harvard University Press. 1987.

CHAPTER 3

1 Carey, John, ed. *Eyewitness to History*. Harvard University Press, 1987.

CHAPTER 4

1 Carey, John, ed. *Eyewitness to History*. Harvard University Press, 1987.

2 Reeves, Richard. *Infamy: The Shocking Story of the Japanese American Internment in World War II*. Henry Holt and Co., 2015.

CHAPTER 5

1 Ward, Geoffrey C. and Burns, Ken. *The War: An Intimate History* 1941–1945. Alfred A. Knopf, 2007.

2 Bradley, James. *Flyboys: A True Story of Courage*, Back Bay Books, 2004.

CHAPTER 6

1 jewishvirtuallibrary.org

2 Carey, John, ed. *Eyewitness to History*. Harvard University Press, 1987.

CHAPTER 7

1 Shephard, Ben. *The Long Road Home: The Aftermath of the Second World War.* Alfred A. Knopf, 2011.

QR CODE GLOSSARY

page 10: fasttrackteaching.com/ffap/Unit_10_WW2/U10_WW2_screen_maps.html

page 10: commons.wikimedia.org/wiki/File:Pacific_Area_-_The_Imperial_Powers_1939_-_Map.svg

page 10: commons.wikimedia.org/wiki/File:Map_of_Africa_in_1939.png

page 15: eyewitnesstohistory.com/w1frm.htm

page 17: youtube.com/watch?v=NESwuWtudtA

page 17: youtube.com/watch?v=tH4zintf6qg

page 22: youtube.com/watch?v=FsynSgeo_Uo&list=PL1mZeR4wTBoxiM86th4lOXhMQN8wDWYAt

page 22: theboot.com/war-songs

page 23: rjgeib.com/thoughts/abraham/abraham.html

page 23: poetryfoundation.org/poems-and-poets/poems/detail/47426

page 23: poetryfoundation.org/articles/70139/the-poetry-of-world-war-i

RESOURCES

page 24: commons.wikimedia.org/wiki/File:A_Battery_Shelled_Art.IWMART2747.jpg

page 24: commons.wikimedia.org/wiki/File:We_are_making_a_new_World_(1918)_(Art._IWM_ART_1146).jpg

page 24: commons.wikimedia.org/wiki/File:Sappers_at_work_-_Canadian_Tunnelling_Company,_R14,_St_Eloi_Art.IWMART2708.jpg

page 24: metmuseum.org/connections/war_and_conflict#/Complete

page 33: eyewitnesstohistory.com/reichstagfire.htm

page 36: youtube.com/watch?v=AnpTWKKWQ1o

page 36: winstonchurchill.org/resources/speeches/1940-the-finest-hour/we-shall-never-surrender

page 44: youtube.com/watch?v=agJLXYRAo_w

page 46: eyewitnesstohistory.com/leningrad.htm

page 50: youtube.com/watch?v=_H3y7klK-uE

page 58: facinghistory.org/nanjing-atrocities/atrocities/i-will-never-forget-voices-survivors

page 61: youtube.com/watch?v=ZDa2h1wBsHk

page 65: tellingstories.org/internment

page 66: history.com/speeches/fdr-asks-congress-to-declare-war-on-japan

page 66: millercenter.org/the-presidency/presidential-speeches

page 67: nebraskastudies.org/0800/frameset_reset.html?http://www.nebraskastudies.org/0800/stories/0801_0107.html

page 67: swarthmore.edu/library/peace/conscientiousobjection/co%20website/pages/HomeNew.htm

page 67: civilianpublicservice.org/people

page 68: army.mil/symbols/enlisteddescriptions.html

page 68: army.mil/symbols/officerdescription.html

page 91: youtube.com/watch?v=0wg5x5WaZPo

page 93: ushmm.org/outreach/en/article.php?ModuleId=10007738

page 93: yadvashem.org/righteous/stories.html

page 101: youtube.com/watch?v=Vy_LIKE9OMQ

page 104: youtube.com/watch?v=fK1MwhEDjHg

page 107: un.org

page 108: pewresearch.org/fact-tank/2016/12/06/just-10-states-resettled-more-than-half-of-recent-refugees-to-u-s

page 108: unhcr.org/en-us/stories.html

page 109: poetryfoundation.org/poems/44266/mending-wall

A

B

C

D

E

F

G

H

INDEX